BFI Film Classics

The BFI Film Classics series introduces, interprets and celebrates landmarks of world cinema. Each volume offers an argument for the film's 'classic' status, together with discussion of its production and reception history, its place within a genre or national cinema, an account of its technical and aesthetic importance, and in many cases, the author's personal response to the film.

For a full list of titles in the series, please visit https://www.bloomsbury.com/uk/series/bfi-film-classics/

T0347691

The Godfather, Part II

Jon Lewis

THE BRITISH FILM INSTITUTE
Bloomsbury Publishing Plc
50 Bedford Square, London, WC1B 3DP, UK
1385 Broadway, New York, NY 10018, USA
29 Earlsfort Terrace, Dublin 2, Ireland

BLOOMSBURY is a trademark of Bloomsbury Publishing Plc

First published in Great Britain 2022 by Bloomsbury on behalf of the
British Film Institute
21 Stephen Street, London W1T 1LN
www.bfi.org.uk

The BFI is the lead organisation for film in the UK and the distributor of Lottery funds for film.
Our mission is to ensure that film is central to our cultural life, in particular by supporting and
nurturing the next generation of filmmakers and audiences. We serve a public role which covers
the cultural, creative and economic aspects of film in the UK.

Copyright © Jon Lewis 2022

Jon Lewis has asserted his right under the Copyright, Designs and Patents Act, 1988,
to be identified as author of this work.

Cover artwork: © Simone Riccardi
Series cover design: Louise Dugdale
Series text design: Ketchup/SE14
Images from *The Godfather, Part II* (Francis Ford Coppola, 1974), © Paramount Pictures Corporation;
The Godfather (Francis Ford Coppola, 1972), © Paramount Pictures Corporation

All rights reserved. No part of this publication may be reproduced or transmitted in any form or
by any means, electronic or mechanical, including photocopying, recording, or any information
storage or retrieval system, without prior permission in writing from the publishers.

Bloomsbury Publishing Plc does not have any control over, or responsibility for, any third-party
websites referred to or in this book. All internet addresses given in this book were correct at the
time of going to press. The author and publisher regret any inconvenience caused if addresses
have changed or sites have ceased to exist, but can accept no responsibility for any such changes.

A catalogue record for this book is available from the British Library.

A catalog record for this book is available from the Library of Congress.

ISBN: PB: 978-1-8390-2326-2
        ePDF: 978-1-8390-2327-9
        ePUB: 978-1-8390-2328-6

Produced for Bloomsbury Publishing Plc by Sophie Contento
Printed and bound in India

To find out more about our authors and books visit www.bloomsbury.com
and sign up for our newsletters.

Contents

Introduction

It is early December 1974: the first public screening of a rough
cut of *The Godfather, Part II*. The site is the director Francis Ford
Coppola's adopted home, San Francisco, and the audience is largely
hand-picked, composed of friends, co-workers and subscribers to
one of the director's many side-projects, *City Magazine*. A lot is
riding on the film – for Coppola and for the studio, Paramount. For
those prone to superstition, and most everyone in Hollywood is, the
warning signs are hard to ignore: the projector breaks four times,
pushing the running time to nearly four hours. When the lights come
up, the audience seems more weary than impressed. One of Coppola's
assistants reads a preview card out loud: 'I hope there will be no
Godfather, Part III,' to which the director adds, 'So do I.'[1]

Coppola takes copious notes and executes over thirty
changes before scheduling a second screening four days later, which
prompts yet more changes. Meanwhile, the director seems oddly
distracted; he has other and bigger things on his mind. He is talking
to the press daily it seems about revolutionising Hollywood, about
someday running a studio of his own. He has a host of ambitious
projects and assets in place or in the works: a magazine, an indie-
distribution outfit (Cinema 5), guaranteed financing as one-third
of Paramount's Directors Company alongside William Friedkin
and Peter Bogdanovich, and a financial stake in a handful of
projects developed at his San Francisco-based production company
American Zoetrope, including *American Graffiti* (a Best Picture
nominee in 1974 and a box-office sensation), *The Conversation*
(which won for Coppola the top prize at Cannes in 1974) and
THX 1138 (which helped launch the considerable career of
George Lucas). Executives at Paramount are actually worried
about Coppola's ruminations on a New Hollywood; such is his

prestige – such is the seeming impact of the auteur renaissance he has set in motion.

The Godfather, Part II premieres in New York in December 1974 and it is everything Coppola has promised it would be; the film achieves a near-perfect balance between art and commerce, pleasing fellow artists, critics, filmgoers and the executives at Paramount. It wins Oscars for Best Picture, Best Director, Best Actor in a Supporting Role, Best Writing, Screenplay Adapted from Other Material, Best Art Direction and Best Music, Original Score. By the time its first run is complete, *The Godfather, Part II* earns a healthy profit as well: close to $60 million in domestic box-office revenues off a $13 million budget.

The widely read *New Yorker* reviewer Pauline Kael, who in 1969 wrote in exasperation that Hollywood had 'devolved into a rotting system in which mediocrity and skyrocketing costs work together to turn out films that would have a hard time making money even if they were good',[2] lauds *The Godfather, Part II* as a turning point for the director and for an emerging New Hollywood: '[*The Godfather, Part II*] is the work of a major artist ... who else, when he got the chance and power, would have proceeded with the absolute conviction that he'd make the film the way it should be made? In movies, that's the inner voice of an authentic hero.'[3] Writing for the *LA Times*, Charles Champlin is similarly effusive: 'The creative, aesthetic success of this long enterprise is, I think, on the heroic scale ... in its way, *Godfather II* is more daring than the original ... [and] the risks were worth taking.'[4]

By the time *The Godfather, Part II* wound up its first run in the late spring of 1975 Coppola was indisputably at the pinnacle of his Hollywood career. But he did not stay there (at the top) for long. Just four years later, he would be the subject of press ridicule when the location shoot of *Apocalypse Now* clocked its 200th day. The director, paraphrasing Euripides, quipped to his co-workers self-effacingly: 'Whom God wishes to destroy, he first makes successful in show business.' The remark proved prophetic. Coppola did not take over Hollywood; but that it seemed on Oscar night 1975 possible he could testifies to the commercial and artistic impact of the first two *Godfather* films.

The development and production of *The Godfather* involved a surfeit of intrigue and conflict.[5] The making of the sequel was a good deal less fraught. Indeed, the mostly cooperative and collaborative development and production of *The Godfather, Part II* rather made the case that an indulgence of an auteur theory – that studio investment in the apparent genius of talented film-makers – might actually work to the benefit of movie-makers and moneymen alike. *The Godfather, Part II* marks the moment when everything seemed perfect for Coppola and for a new generation of film-makers ... just before things would never be so perfect for any of them again.

The Godfather, Part II proved to be a turning point in the New Hollywood because it was also the turning point in the career of the industry's premier player: Francis Coppola. The director navigated the 1970s American film business expertly. In the space of seven years, he directed three box-office blockbusters (and was credited with a fourth as executive producer), received two Palmes d'Or at Cannes, netted twelve Academy Award nominations (as producer, director and screenwriter) and took home five Oscar statuettes. His many side-projects – the magazine, the indie distribution and production units, the Directors Company experiment at Paramount and later his purchase of the Hollywood General Studio lot in 1980 – at first blush evinced the scale and scope of his ambition, but they also set the stage for his comeuppance: 'whom God wishes to destroy', and all that. In 1974, Coppola was Hollywood's most famous, most important director. And *The Godfather, Part II* – the film under review here – is the reason why.

1 The Godfather Business

Plans for a sequel were first mooted in the summer of 1972 just as it became clear how good the box-office returns on *The Godfather* would be. The Paramount Studios marketing team had managed the release of the first *Godfather* film brilliantly, creating demand by under-supplying the market, opening in just a handful of theatres in key markets. Newspapers reported on the long lines outside these theatres, proclaiming *The Godfather* as not just a movie, but an event. Much as Paramount needed a sequel, they needed Coppola to direct it. But the young auteur was hardly keen on the prospect; he had in more than one interview referred to the project as 'Abbott and Costello Meet the Godfather'.

The most significant obstacle to Paramount's plan was the relationship between the studio production chief Robert Evans and Coppola. Both men were after 1972 at career crossroads. Both wanted to prove themselves successful without the other. That said, a *Godfather* sequel had an undeniable, irresistible, practical appeal for either or both of them to further build their reputations and to cash in one last time on a sure thing. Studio president Frank Yablans planned to use the sequel to buoy his career too, and to help launch The Directors Company, a 'specialty division' at Paramount created to exploit the talents of three young film-makers: Coppola, Bogdanovich (who had just directed the Oscar-nominated *Last Picture Show* in 1971) and Friedkin (an Oscar winner in 1972 for *The French Connection*). In exchange for hitching their talents to the studio brand, these three film-makers received secured and guaranteed financing, studio distribution and a degree of creative autonomy.

The Directors Company seemed like a good idea, but using *The Godfather, Part II* to launch it never gained traction at Gulf and Western (which owned Paramount). In the end, the unit laid claim to only three films: Coppola's *The Conversation* (a critical success), Bogdanovich's *Paper Moon* (a box-office success in 1973 for which Tatum O'Neill won a Best Supporting Actress Oscar) and *Daisy Miller* (a film Bogdanovich made in 1974 with his then girlfriend Cybill Shepherd miscast in the lead; a bomb at the box office widely panned by movie critics).

Another glitch in the development of the sequel involved Oscar night 1973 and what should have been good news at Paramount: a Best Actor win for Marlon Brando. The story goes something like this. On the evening of 27 March 1973 at the actor's house on Mulholland Drive, a 26-year-old Native American activist named Sacheen Littlefeather – she would later be rumoured to be a hired actor, a Mexican imposter or a stripper – met with Brando to discuss a document he had just composed: a verbose Oscar acceptance speech she would read on his behalf if he won. Littlefeather was at the time working as a public service director for a San Francisco radio station, heading as well a local affirmative action committee. While hiking the hills near her home months before Oscar night, she befriended one of the neighbourhood's budding celebrities, Francis Ford Coppola. She had heard from her friends in the social justice/ affirmative action communities that Brando, the star of Coppola's popular film and a politically progressive Hollywood celebrity, might be enlisted to help her cause. So, she summoned the courage to ask Coppola to introduce her to Brando. The young director complied, never guessing at what a bad idea that would turn out to be.

With Brando's personal assistant in tow, Littlefeather arrived at the ceremony in a tasselled buckskin dress and moccasins; her straight black hair adorned at the temples with a feathered headdress. She was barely in the door before the show's director, Howard Koch, took her aside and told her she would not be permitted to read Brando's eight-page speech. He would allow her no more than sixty seconds on stage.

For those on hand at the Dorothy Chandler Pavilion in Los Angeles, and for the 85 million watching on television, what followed proved to be a memorable sixty seconds. Unable to read from the

Sacheen Littlefeather declining Marlon Brando's Oscar in 1973 (Bettmann/Getty Images)

lengthy script, Littlefeather extemporised: Brando had decided not to accept the award, she said, 'because of the treatment of American Indians today by the film industry and on television and movie reruns … and also with the recent happenings at Wounded Knee'. Amidst a mixed bag of applause, jeers and baffled laughter, Littlefeather concluded by expressing Brando's fervent hope that 'in the future, our hearts and understandings will meet with love and generosity'.[6] She kept to Koch's time limit and got off the stage a few seconds before John Wayne could get onto it.

Two months later on his TV talk show, Dick Cavett asked Brando, 'If you had the Academy Awards night to do over again, would you do any of it differently?' Brando paused and then, amidst nervous laughter, his eyes rolling skyward, uttered a single syllable: 'Well …'. More laughter. Having established the fact he was among friends: 'I don't think so, no. I felt that there was an opportunity, since the American Indian hasn't been able to hear his voice heard, or have his voice heard, anywhere in the United States, I felt it was a marvellous opportunity for an Indian to voice his opinion to 85 million people.'

Although 'the stunt' seemed at the time a bit obtuse as acts of rebellion go, it is hard today to resist a bit of easy wordplay and to insist that there was a Method to Brando's apparent madness. Wounded Knee was the site of an 1890 massacre of American Indians by white colonial forces, a town nearly a century later occupied in protest by approximately 200 Oglala Lakota. The February 1973 protest prompted a standoff between the activists and federal agents. And although Littlefeather's speech on behalf of Brando surely seemed weird, it got seen and talked about. And it ended an inexcusable media silence on the events happening at Wounded Knee.

Brando was after Oscar night deemed off-limits for the sequel, so Coppola, who agreed to work with Mario Puzo on a script for the sequel, worked up

this crazy idea of a movie that would be two time periods that would tell the story of the father and the son when they were the same age. You would see Michael when he was a mature young man and, of course, the father, who would have been already dead. It was far out but I liked it.

Paramount liked the script idea too. Still, Coppola refused to direct the sequel:

I went to them and I said, 'We have a script and I'll tell you the director who should do it … This young director, I think is a fabulous talent …' They said, 'Fine, who is he?' I said, 'Martin Scorsese.' They said, 'Absolutely not. That's outrageous.' So I told them to forget it. Goodbye. Then the whole deal was off.

Then, as Coppola recalled years later:

Charlie Bluhdorn [the CEO of Gulf and Western] himself calls me up, with his Viennese accent. 'Francis, you are crazy. You're not going to do it? You have the formula of Coca-Cola. You're not going to make more Coca-Cola?' I said, 'Charlie, my opinion of Bob Evans, he has talent but he was so tough on me and he's so second-guessing of me, it's such a struggle, I don't want to go through it again.' ... I said, 'OK, here's my deal. One, I want a million dollars. That's to write and direct it.' That to me was like asking for a great fortune. 'Number two, I want Bob Evans to have nothing to do with it. I don't have to talk to him. He doesn't read the script. I don't get his opinions. And number three, I don't want to call it some stupid sequel. I want to call it *The Godfather, Part II.*'

Bluhdorn acceded right away on the first two demands – the million dollars and the banishment of Evans (with whom Bluhdorn had other problems, anyway). 'But we can't call the picture *The Godfather, Part II.*' Coppola asked why not. Bluhdorn replied: 'Because our marketing department tells us that if we call the movie *The Godfather, Part II* everyone's going to think it's the second half of the movie they already saw instead of a separate movie.'[7] As things would play out, Coppola eventually got his way on the third demand as well.

In a 1975 *Playboy* interview, just as *The Godfather, Part II* had become a critical and box-office success, Coppola reflected upon his decision to direct the film:

It seemed such a terrible idea that I began to be intrigued ... Sometimes I sit around thinking I'd like to get a job directing a TV soap opera, just to see if I could make it the most wonderful thing of its kind ever done. Or I imagine devoting myself to directing the plays of a cub-scout troop and having it be the most exciting theater in the country ... when something seems so outrageous, you just have to do it.

Although he had by then directed two of the highest-grossing films in Hollywood history, in 1975 Coppola made clear he did not want to become part of the Hollywood machine, a studio director in the old Hollywood sense: 'As you become big, you get absorbed.' But he was aware as well of the risks of his artistic ambition: 'The artist's worst fear is that he'll be exposed as a sham.'[8]

From the advent of his film-making career, Coppola's considerable ambition and penchant for risk was worn tantalisingly on his sleeve. And at the core of even his most egregious boasts was

a 1960s film school catechism – an investment in the auteur theory.
Fresh out of UCLA in 1968, Coppola announced: 'I don't think there
will be a Hollywood as we know it when this generation of film
students gets out of college.'[9] The following year, on Warner Bros.'
dime, he set out to make that happen. Under the American Zoetrope
banner, Coppola moved to San Francisco with a cadre of recent
film school grads, including George Lucas, John Milius and Carroll
Ballard, and started talking about remaking Hollywood.

The executives at Warner Bros. failed to appreciate what
Coppola's crew had on offer – in development: *American Graffiti*,
Apocalypse Now, *The Conversation* and *THX 1138* ... films that
would help shape the auteur renaissance. When the Warner Bros.
development deal unravelled in 1970, Coppola pondered his future:
'I felt like someone starting the first air-mail run from Kansas to
Omaha ... In ten years, the giants of the film industry are going to be
companies that are so small no one has ever heard of them.'[10] He was
right about the change, dead wrong about the details.

After film school, Coppola worked his way up through the
ranks, within the system. Like Bogdanovich and Scorsese, he worked
for Sam Arkoff and Roger Corman at American International (AIP),
then hit the big time as a screenwriter for hire, winning an Oscar for
his work on Richard Nixon's favourite film, *Patton* (1970). 'The way
to come to power is not always to merely challenge the establishment,
but first to make a place within it and then challenge and double
cross the establishment.'[11] In 1972, looking back on his dealings with
Paramount during the production of *The Godfather*:

You are never going to take over an industry with your back turned to it ...
You can't just shake your fist at the establishment and put them down for
not giving you the chance. You have to beat them down and take that money
from them ... You have to set your sights and be unscrupulous.[12]

In an interview with Marjorie Rosen for *Film Comment* in 1975,
Coppola mused at his sudden celebrity: 'You've got to understand

Francis Coppola at American Zoetrope HQ in 1970 (Bettmann/Getty Images)

that all I have done for thirteen years is try to have a career. I went right from school to film school and here I am without ever stopping.' He was not yet 33 years old when the first *Godfather* film came out; 36 when he won Best Director for the sequel. He had learned on the fly and on the job. Surviving and surmounting the bickering, the subterfuge and the grandstanding that characterised the development and production of *The Godfather* afforded Coppola the – and this word is chosen carefully here – *authority* he desired for the sequel. By then, things surely seemed to be going according to plan. 'I don't need to work for money anymore,' Coppola boasted, making reference to a familiar *Godfather* backstory – that he didn't initially want to direct *The Godfather* and that Lucas had to talk him into it, promising that if he made the film Paramount wanted him to make, he'd never have to direct another studio film. 'I may not make any more films,' he told Rosen. 'I don't know. Anything I do will be just what I think of.'

Contrary to popular misconception, Coppola did not do the sequel for money; he did it to achieve what every self-respecting late-1960s film school student dreamed of:

I began to think of letting *The Godfather* format subsidize me in doing
something more ambitious in the sequel than they wanted ... *Godfather II*
falls more into the category of a personal film, although it cost twelve million
dollars [a lot for 1974; and $4 million more than the first film].[13]

The sequel offered Coppola the opportunity to assert his auteur
signature; to build upon what the first film established: the stylistic
tendencies, the thematic preoccupations. It offered as well the
opportunity to extend the Corleone saga into the past and future –
flashing back to turn-of-the-century Sicily and New York, to postwar
Tahoe, Havana and Washington DC – to embellish and comment
upon the gangster-capitalist parable introduced in the first film: the
Corleone family saga as a commentary on American aspiration and
assimilation; as a metaphor for American capitalism (and capitalists),
the corruption of American power, this time fully post-Vietnam and,
more trenchantly and recently, post-Watergate. 'My father is not so
different from other powerful men,' Michael tells Kay when he courts
her for a second time after his exile in Sicily in *The Godfather*. Her
knee-jerk reply is that such a notion is 'naïve', but Coppola spends
the last ninety minutes of the first film and three hours plus of the
second to over and again prove Michael right.

'My father is not so
different from other
powerful men'
(*The Godfather*)

2 A Movie of Meetings

The Godfather, Part II is a gorgeous, stylised, auteur epic – this despite the fact that the film is comprised almost entirely of meetings: Michael and Senator Geary, Michael and Frankie Pentangeli, Michael and Hyman Roth, Michael and the many investors in Cuban economic development, Michael and his brother Fredo, Michael and his mother, Michael and his attorney Tom Hagen, Michael and his wife Kay, Michael and his sister Connie, Vito and the crime boss Fannuci, Vito and the landlord, Vito and Don Francesco, Tom and Pentangeli … The meetings remind us that the modern gangster's success is built upon inside information and on strategic planning. Vito's and Michael's days resemble those of the legitimate businessmen they aspire or pretend to be.

The narrative structure – this movie of meetings – is a challenge Coppola surmounts with a meticulous, theatrical *mise en scène*: long takes, low-contrast, chiaroscuro lighting; theatrical blocking (highlighting gesture, line delivery and especially performance; a lot depends on his cast and their ability to inhabit what had become for the American filmgoing public a familiar family, a familiar world). To establish continuity between the past and future – beginning with Vito's arrival in New York from Sicily, on through Michael's continued consolidation and expansion of power after Vito's death – Coppola opted for an old-fashioned optical effect: the dissolve – a visual effect in which one image slowly fades out as another slowly fades in. The dissolve is a characteristically 'soft' transitional, editorial device – well suited to the film's leisurely pace and to Coppola's theatrical *mise en scène*. (The dissolve simulates the mechanical lowering and raising of scrims in stage-craft. In Coppola's 1982 film *One from the Heart*, he took the technique one step further, combining artful dissolves with mechanically manipulated

constructed sets and scrims.) The optical figure implies as well
an easy logic to the family and corporate succession – from Vito
to Michael.

The Godfather, Part II begins with Michael alone at his Lake
Tahoe compound. It's a neat bit of foreshadowing; this is a film about
what happens, but also about *how* and *why*. We cut to a scene set a
half-century earlier: the Corleone origin story and Vito Andolini in
Sicily in 1901. Vito is 9 years old and attends with his mother the
funeral of his father, who has been assassinated over a slight to a local
gangster. Vito's brother Paolo has sworn revenge and has gone into
hiding in the hills. There is a procession reminiscent of the courtship
scene between Michael and Apollonia in *The Godfather* – the first of
many such allusions to the first film.

The procession is interrupted by news of the murder of Paolo.
We cut to Vito's mother as she pleads with Don Francesco at his

Vito's mother
holds a knife to
Don Francesco's
throat and then is
murdered as Vito
makes his escape

estate; she refers to her last living son (Vito – the future Godfather) as 'dumb-witted' and adds for good measure, 'he never speaks'. But the Don figures Vito will grow up, and when he does, he will seek his vengeance. Vito runs, and when his mother shields his exit a shotgun blasts her from on to off screen.

Vito escapes and a dissolve takes us from an empty street in Corleone, Sicily, to the prow of the *Moshulu*, a ship headed to New York harbour. Indulging an allusion to Chaplin's *The Immigrant* (1917), a shot of the ship as it passes Liberty Island cues a pan across the anxious faces of the sundry immigrants. On Ellis Island Vito gets a new surname – the name we know him by: Corleone. It is a mistake made by an impatient intake officer, but it nonetheless grounds him as the product of a place and culture he has crossed an ocean to escape. This will not be the last time in the film the family name will be mistaken, mispronounced.

The future Godfather is a scrawny pre-teen who, as his mother suggested, is mostly mute. Quarantined on Ellis Island, he pauses at a dirty window and gazes into the distance. A reflection of Lady Liberty appears alongside his face. We cut from a tight shot of the window to a wider shot of his room. As Vito gazes out of the window, we for the first time hear his voice as he sings to himself in pre-adolescent soprano. The song forms a sound bridge – a technique Coppola uses a lot in the film – that accompanies a dissolve, from (as a title supers) 'Vito Corleone, Ellis Island 1901' to Anthony, Michael and Kay's

Vito Corleone
on Ellis Island

son, in Tahoe at his confirmation. The sound bridge (of Vito singing) persists through the dissolve, then diminishes in favour of the live sound of the Tahoe church. Anthony looks a lot like young Vito; the 'Sicilian thing that's been going on for 2,000 years' that Kay will later lament.

The reception that follows recalls Connie's wedding, and Coppola does well to exploit the interior/exterior, business/family dualities that are also in play in the opening half hour of *The Godfather*. The dignitaries who send Vito their apologies in the first film have this time shown up, notably Senator Geary, who during the requisite photo op mispronounces Michael's surname: 'Cor-le-on' – three syllables, not four, anglicising the Italian. Geary seems a bumbler; we figure, a Nevada hick.

Unlike Connie's wedding – an Italian affair from start to finish – in Tahoe there are overt gestures at assimilation. Michael is dressed in a light, summer-weight suit. There are plenty of WASPs at the reception, not just hard guys in sunglasses. The Sierra Boys Choir – an all-WASP outfit – commence singing an American pop song: 'Mr Wonderful', a little wink or joke that provides a sound cue to a cut, this time from outside to in, to Michael (our 'Mr Wonderful') in his home office. We enter the scene late, just as Geary is shaking Michael down: 'Let's cut the bullshit; I don't want to spend any more time here than I have to … you can have the [casino] licence – the price is $250,000.' We cut from Michael listening to Geary to Tom gazing back at Michael to read *his* reaction, a first hint at Tom's diminished status in the family business. Geary presses his luck, '… plus 5 per cent of the gross from all of the hotels, Mr Cor-le-own-ee [four syllables, not three]'.

Michael's eyes go cold: 'Now the price for the licence is $20,000, am I right? Now why would I ever consider paying more than that?' Geary: 'Because I intend to squeeze you … I don't like your kind of people … trying to pass yourselves off as decent Americans … I despise your masquerade.' The struggle over assimilation – a theme in the first film; an even bigger issue in the

Senator Geary in Michael's office

sequel – seems for the moment beside the point, as Michael delivers
the scene's payoff: 'Senator, we're both part of the same hypocrisy ...'.
Here, for the first but not last time, we are brought back to Michael's
musings about powerful men, a reference in the first *Godfather*
film to Vietnam but here a necessary allusion to what Nixon and
Watergate (which has transpired in the meantime between the two
films) have done to collective assumptions about powerful men
in America. For Michael, there is no power without corruption;
no power without crime. Michael is a gangster. And following his
reasoning, so is Geary. So is Nixon.

Geary disregards Michael's musings on moral relativism. A neat
bit of props-work heightens the tension as G. D. Spradlin, who plays
Geary, takes a moment to point a toy cannon at Al Pacino/Michael.
Coppola shoots Geary's exit in a single shot. He stops to shake Kay's
hand – another masquerade, worth noting, as he has only moments
earlier insulted her. Coppola uses variable focus to guide our rooting
interests: Geary and his entourage move out of focus while Al Neri,

Michael's henchman, occupies the foreground very much in focus.
The technique offers little doubt about who will win and who will
not. A subsequent cut to Michael in medium close-up is followed
by a cut to Tom, also in medium close-up. Both remain seated and
neither see any reason to follow Geary out. They are done with
the masquerade.

A hard cut to a long shot of the party takes us from the dark
confines of Michael's office to the reception on the shore of the
lake. There, Michael's older brother Fredo is greeted by Frankie
Pentangeli – the two family members who will betray Michael.
'He has me waiting in the lobby!' Pentangeli fumes. Later, we
may well look back on this moment and think that Michael has
miscalculated here. Why has he so antagonised Pentangeli? But the
problem is in the end Pentangeli's not Michael's, whose grander
plans require patience, something neither Fredo nor Pentangeli have
much of. Michael keeps them both at arm's length, a matter rendered
physical/visual as the two men are kept waiting outside.

Fredo (right) with Frankie Pentangeli (centre) and Willi Cicci

A tonal cut from light to dark marks the arrival in Michael's office of Johnny Ola, who is not made to wait in the lobby. Michael dismisses Tom – another suggestion of his diminished status. Ola, we discover, works for 'our man in Miami', the gangster Hyman Roth. Ola and Michael shake on the casino deal. Situated back to back, the two meetings make clear that Michael doesn't need Geary's permission to make moves in Nevada, but he does need Roth's.

We cut back to the party outside. And back to the theme of assimilation and its role in the evolution of Michael's family business. Pentangeli tries to get the band to play an Italian song. He sings the backbeat but no one in the band recognises the song. The clarinetist plays 'Pop Goes the Weasel'. Pentangeli wonders aloud where all the Italians have gone. It's a fair question. Meanwhile, in Michael's office, it's Connie's turn. She has come to ask for money. She's impatient too, and before long she says what has been on Fredo's and Pentangeli's minds as well: 'You're not my father [you're not Vito Corleone].' Michael, ever the pragmatist, sees no point in taking offence: 'So what do you come to me for?'

That a mob boss might have family problems like the rest of us civilians is what the TV producer David Chase used so well to make Michael's small-screen heir Tony Soprano identifiable, even sympathetic. Tony's business enterprise was throughout *The Sopranos* interrupted by domestic problems: a jealous wife, wacky teenagers, a cranky uncle, a malevolent mother. Tony tries to be everything to everyone and, as things play out in so many domestic melodramas, he ends up satisfying no one – he ends up with an anxiety disorder that sends him into therapy. With Michael it's harder to feel empathy because he so completely compartmentalises family life, because he deals with his family only when they interfere with business. He makes his business life better and his domestic life simpler by killing his brother-in-law and his older brother and by sending his wife away. We may admire the simplicity and efficiency – more on that later – but we recognise as well that we'd never be so ruthless, that we'd never be him.

Connie leaves and Pentangeli finally gets an audience. The film highlights waiting; we are made aware of narrative time, screen time, real time. Patience is a virtue, and it is for Michael a winning strategy. Pentangeli and Michael converse, in Italian at first, about Pentangeli's problems with Roth. Pentangeli is family; he lives, we later discover, in what was once Vito's house. But such ties bind only so much and Pentangeli's impatience threatens Michael's bottom line: 'I have business that is important with Hyman Roth. I don't want it disturbed.' Pentangeli is still riled by the all-WASP band and the 'can-o-peas' (as he pronounces canapés) he's been served as appetisers (instead of sausages and peppers) and vents his resistance to Michael's larger, less family-based vision of mob business. He asks point blank: 'You give your loyalty to a Jew before your own blood?' Michael rolls his eyes. From his vantage point, the question is ridiculous, naïve. 'Come on, Frankie, you know my father did business with Hyman Roth. He respected him.' Pentangeli shouts his response: 'Your father did business with Hyman Roth. Your father respected Hyman Roth. But your father never trusted Hyman Roth. Or his Sicilian messenger boy Johnny Ola.'

Coppola gives Pentangeli the scene's payoff or exit line, but it is neatly undercut as ironic, a mode of rhetoric of little use in the sombre and serious business of Mafia capitalism: 'There's not going to be no trouble from me, Don Corleone.' The line just sits in the air. The scene ends not with Pentangeli's exit and exit line but with a cut to the ever-present Neri, who recognises the slight. Later he will ask Michael, 'You want [Pentangeli] to leave?' And he doesn't just mean the party.

Pacino's performance here, especially as the confirmation party scene so resembles the wedding that opens *The Godfather*, proved crucial to establishing a continuity from the first film to the sequel. Pacino was always going to be vital to the sequel. But getting him on board proved difficult.

Options tying actors to sequels are pro forma today, but they were not in 1971 when *The Godfather* was first cast. In 1973,

Paramount had to negotiate anew with Pacino for the sequel and the actor harboured a grudge; he felt he had been underpaid on the first film. And he wanted to move on with his career. Paramount executives made matters worse with an initial low-ball offer of $100,000 – a lot of money in the real world in 1973 and nearly triple what the actor had been paid for the first film. Better offers followed, but none of them good enough to change the actor's mind.

With the sequel's start date approaching, Pacino agreed to meet with studio executives in New York. There was – and everyone could agree on this – no film without him. 'There was a bottle of J&B on the table,' Pacino recalled years later:

We began drinking, talking, laughing, and the producer opened his drawer and he pulled out a tin box. I was sitting on the other side and he pushed it over in my direction. He said, 'What if I were to tell you that there was $1,000,000 in cash there?'

The symmetry with offers one can't refuse was intentional. Still Pacino baulked. Then Coppola stepped in. And sealed the deal:

Francis told me about the script. He was so wigged out by the prospect of doing it, he would inspire anybody. The hairs on my head stood up ... if you feel that from a director, go with him ... I left [the meeting] absolutely filled with his inspiration.[14]

For the record, Pacino signed for $600,000 plus 10 points on the net.

Once the financial details were settled, Pacino read the script and began to worry at the evolution of his character: 'Michael has to start out ambivalent [in *The Godfather*], almost unsure of himself and his place.' Pacino notes, 'He's caught between his Old World family and the postwar American Dream.'[15] The first film ends as Michael orders and witnesses the murder of his brother-in-law Carlo because he recognises its importance to his ascendance. It is a decisive act, a symbolic act, a quasi-biblical sacrifice. He orders the murder of

Tessio as well, one of his father's lieutenants, to show that he quite literally 'means business'.

At the start of the second film, Michael has learned to live with these decisions; he has, as Ron Rosenbaum writes in *Vanity Fair*, 'killed everything human inside himself for the sake of the abstract honor of the family'.[16] The first film ends with the door slowly shutting Kay out. The expression on her face is hard to read. It is fair to wonder what Coppola asked Diane Keaton to do or show us in the take he used. Far clearer is what her gesture reveals about Michael, who has, however reluctantly, acceded to the demands of his new position as CEO of the New York Mafia. The sequel features a similar scene meant to have a similar effect – a second scene of a door shutting Kay out of his life. Pacino struggled to find the right mood, the right preparation for the scene. He listened to some Stravinsky. He worked on moving 'all heavy', so it would appear as if his character was accommodating some terrible burden. And then he found one last bit of inspiration on the costumier's rack: an expensive camel hair coat. There was a 'funereal casualness' to the garment, Pacino recalled, 'that remove[d] Michael in a way ... something distant ...'.[17]

A lot has been made over the years about Pacino's *Method*, but Pacino doesn't see himself as a Method actor, as he doesn't rely much on sense memory.[18] He uses instead improvisations drawing from fictional and real-world characters, text sources, everyday topics. For his now legendary Actors Studio audition, Pacino chose a monologue

The 'funereal casualness' of Pacino's camel hair coat

from Eugene O'Neill's *The Iceman Cometh*, which he used as a set-up for a soliloquy from *Hamlet*. The audience applauded – unusual, and frankly frowned upon at the school. Actors Studio director Lee Strasberg (who plays Hyman Roth in *The Godfather, Part II*) asked Pacino to switch things up: Hickey (from *Iceman*) doing Hamlet, then Hamlet delivering Hickey's lines. Strasberg had, he thought, seen it all before; well, he'd seen plenty (from Brando, Montgomery Clift, Marilyn Monroe, Shelley Winters). But after Pacino finished the audition, Strasberg felt compelled to comment aloud: 'The courage you have shown today is rarer than talent.'

To play the Cuban-born gangster Tony Montana in *Scarface* (1983), Pacino drew from the macho swagger of the Panamanian boxer Roberto Duran (a smart, and perhaps obvious choice) *and* Meryl Streep's portrait of an émigré traumatised by the world around her in *Sophie's Choice* (1982). For one of the takes of a monologue at the climax of *The Devil's Advocate* (1997), Pacino, playing the devil as a senior partner in a New York law firm, went off script and into a rendition of Sinatra's 'It Happened in Monterey'. The actor Helen Mirren happened to be on the set that day: 'It [was] just absolutely out there ... surreal, brilliant.'

Discussing his craft with the *New Yorker* theatre critic John Lahr, Pacino mused abstractly that acting is about 'getting into a state that brings about freedom and expression and the unconscious'. Adapting Strasberg's teachings, an actor needs to render exterior (what we see and hear) something real that is inside of them, inside their character. Life and art are not indistinguishable, but the overlaps can be useful. 'Some actors *play* characters,' Strasberg notes. 'Al Pacino *becomes* them' (italics in original). For *The Godfather*, Pacino worked *with* the pressures of what was surely his big Hollywood break. His character struggles to live up to the expectations of his father, played by Pacino's idol, Brando. For the sequel, he had Strasberg. The teacher–pupil relationship figured into Pacino's performance, especially as Michael endeavours to impress and finally outsmart Roth.

Pacino allows that there is a bit of Michael inside him: the loneliness ('I always feel that way'), the social anxiety (so many actors are by nature shy). For Pacino, Michael is not a simple villain: 'I didn't see Michael as a gangster ... I saw his struggle as something that was connected to his intelligence, that innate sense of what's around and being able to adjust to things ... The power of the character was in his enigmatic quality. And I thought, well, how do you get to that? I think you wear it inside yourself.'[19]

When Coppola pitched Michael to Pacino during rehearsals for the first film, he told him to imagine 'a young, slightly insecure, naïve and brilliant young college student ... becoming this horrible Mafia killer'. Coppola had less useful advice for the sequel, except to say that the character's evolution was mostly done with: 'he's the same man from beginning to end ... The entire performance had to be kind of vague and so understated that, as an actor, you couldn't really be sure what you were doing.'[20]

The Godfather begins with Connie's wedding reception – an outdoor family party Vito mostly misses as he attends to business inside. Michael also attends to business before venturing outside to enjoy Anthony's party. When he finally surfaces and dances with Kay, she reminds him of his promise to her that the family business would be 100 per cent legitimate in five years ... and that that was seven years ago. 'I'm trying,' he replies. But it's fair to conclude, he really isn't anymore. Legitimacy is tied to assimilation in the first film. That's why Michael goes to college, enlists in the Marines. It is why he insists to Kay, 'That's my father [the gangster who makes offers a bandleader can't refuse], not me.' He'd be on firm ground still maintaining the truth of such a claim: he is not his father, but not because they have different occupations and not because he is a less ruthless Mafiosi.

Michael rationalises gangster capitalism as an aspect of the 'same hypocrisy' that attends all aspiration, ambition, assimilation, capitalist accumulation ... all things being equal in the lives of all successful American men. It is unlikely Vito needed philosophy to rationalise his embrace of and route through the American Dream. Both Vito and Michael balance work and family, especially as they overlap in their line of work so complexly. And while Vito is better at maintaining a balance, Coppola in a 1975 interview reminds us that, setting aside precisely what these men do for a living, success can be rough on relationships: 'I've strung my own wife along for 13 years by telling her that as soon as I was done with this or that project, I'd stop working so hard and we'd live a more normal life. I mean, that's the classic way husbands lie.'[21]

Pacino's Michael evinces a character study suited to the film's period piece: he's a 1950s gangster posing as a 1950s businessman. We see very little of his life outside the office, outside of business – a reversal of the 1950s movie trend showing men at home and at play, while their work lives are summarised as a vague mix of martinis, phone calls and flirtations with secretaries. We see just enough of Michael off duty to know that everyday family problems fall heavily upon him – we see so little of his family life because he mostly avoids it, because he sees it as a distraction from the job at hand. One of the film's rare domestic scenes occurs just as Anthony's party ends and we find Michael and Kay alone together in their bedroom. It's a brief scene packed with information. 'Michael,' Kay asks, half asleep, 'why are the drapes open?' The answer comes not from him but from outside the window: gunfire. Michael pulls Kay off the bed and shields her with his body. Whatever their struggles as a couple, his instinct is to protect her. If we're wondering whether Michael is still in love with Kay, if he is capable of loving anyone, the gesture provides an answer. And this is not the first time he has been tasked with protecting her. Geary's remark about Michael's 'masquerade' included an insult directed at Kay: '[I despise] the dishonest way you pose yourself – you and your whole fucking family.' The breaching of boundaries (the insult, the hit) is disconcerting, unfair.

(*Next page*) Michael protects Kay during the Tahoe assassination attempt

After Michael promotes Tom to interim CEO, a job thanks to actor Robert Duvall's body language we know Tom doesn't want long term, the camera lingers on a medium shot of Michael in profile, screen left foreground. A title supers: 'Vito Corleone New York City 1917', as we dissolve to a deep-focus shot of the Corleone family at the advent of their New York adventure. Vito is sixteen years older than the last time we saw him, and is played now by Robert De Niro. His wife, 'Mama Corleone' (that's the only name she gets in the script and in the film), hovers over a child restless in the foreground in a crib. We dissolve, following him and leaving her behind, to an Italian-language theatre in Little Italy. An actor sings a song about missing the old country. The theatre scene introduces in low angle a new antagonist, Don Fanucci – 'the Black Hand'. He is the bad gangster and Vito will become in his place a new and improved version – a good gangster.

At the theatre, Vito stumbles upon a crime – Fanucci shaking down the company manager. Later, minding his business at home, a crime stumbles upon him. Clemenza drops off some guns and Vito is tasked with hiding them. It's a deal he can't refuse. And it comes at a propitious time as an unlucky chain of events have compelled Vito the former deli clerk to find another line of work. It is with this random act of complicity, this quirk of destiny, that Vito becomes a gangster.

For the early twentieth-century New York City scenes, the cinematographer Gordon Willis kept things dark and dingy, with underpowered naked light bulbs doubling (soon enough, significantly) as props and partial light sources. The tenements are coded in browns and yellows – a lighting and colour scheme smartly adapted in variation for the interiors at the Corleone compounds. Willis's consistency with the city settings makes possible a tonal cut that highlights the transition from the city to the sunlit suburbs as Clemenza and Vito drive off to pick up a carpet – compensation, we gather, for hiding the guns. Clemenza tells Vito he knows the owner of the house, but when they find no one home, he jimmies the front

Clemenza, gun drawn

door lock. To make sure we know that Vito knows that Clemenza has again made him an accomplice to a crime, Coppola stages a little inside/outside set piece. By chance, a cop comes to the door just as the men roll up the rug. Clemenza gestures for Vito's silence and then stands hidden at the doorway, gun drawn. Lucky for everyone in the scene, the cop lingers for a moment at the door but then leaves safe and sound.

Sound-cued by a train whistle, an abrupt cut takes us from Vito to Michael, seated on a train and captured again in profile. His stoic bodyguard, played by the incomparable Amerigo Tot, sits silently with him. The ominous underscoring seems at first a poor match for their destination, a first look at sunlit Miami. But once Michael meets with Roth in his modest bungalow, we realise that the underscoring is not ironic or misleading. Michael has come, or so he says, to get permission to whack Pentangeli, whom he says he blames for the attempt to assassinate him in Tahoe. Roth wanders off subject and talks instead about their plans for the future together.

The incomparable
Amerigo Tot

Frankie Pentangeli
in NYC

Michael insists on the matter at hand: 'So, Pentangeli is a dead man – you don't object?' Pentangeli is 'small potatoes', Roth replies. Top-down gangster capitalism.

Another tonal cut takes us from the conversation about assassination in sunny Miami to snowy New York and the hit's supposed target, Pentangeli. The continuity cutting tracks Michael's linear train of thought. And as Coppola is finally picking up the pace of the editing, we gather Michael is thinking and acting fast. 'It was Hyman Roth who tried to have me killed.' This comes out of nowhere and right after he's got permission from Roth to whack the man he is speaking to. We wonder what Michael is playing at. And Coppola has not clued us in – as if Michael knows things even he, Coppola that is, doesn't know. Michael asks Pentangeli for a favour: make peace with the (Roth-backed) Rosato brothers because it will look to Roth that Michael still trusts him. Michael wants Roth to let down his guard long enough to learn who in his inner circle ratted him out, who helped stage the hit in Tahoe.

Coppola doesn't make us wait, as the next cut reveals the rat to us; and for once, we know something Michael doesn't. We see Fredo at home awakened by a phone call. 'Johnny, Jesus Christ what time … whaddya calling me here for? … I don't know anything – you got me in deep enough already … you guys lied to me. I don't want you calling me anymore …'.

We cut to a bar in New York. Things are happening fast; turns out, too fast for Michael. Pentangeli is targeted by assassins. A cut establishes what we gather is happening in the meantime; an apparent nod to the baptism montage from *The Godfather*, which match-cuts the preparations for and then execution of a series of murders. Geary wakes as if from a bad dream. He is in a whorehouse. A moving camera follows him to a bed, on which we find a bloody corpse. Coppola blocks and dresses the scene strategically. The camera pauses as Geary shares the frame with the dead woman. A mirror at the head of the bed adds an eerie doubling of the corpse. Is Geary responsible for what's happened to this poor

woman or has he been set up? We don't know because it really
doesn't matter.

Neri moves wordlessly in the background. His ubiquity
reflects Michael's reach, a reminder of how much gets done for
Michael without him having to leave the office. Neri ducks in and
then out. Maybe *he* killed the prostitute. All that matters in Geary's
world is how things look. And this looks bad. Tom is there too:
'This girl has no family … it's as if she never existed.' The line played
differently in 1974 than it does today, as some contemporary viewers,
including many of my students, see Tom's speech as dismissive of
the working woman on the bed, dismissive of women in general.
I think we need to be careful here not to overfreight the death of
this prostitute – a character, it is worth noting, we never meet alive.
She's expendable, Tom makes that clear, but not because she's a
woman, and not because she's a sex worker. She's expendable because
she's an outsider, a civilian, a working (excuse the pun) stiff. The
scene ends as Tom offers Geary an alibi in exchange for his loyalty.
We assume Geary accepts the offer. Because he can't refuse. Tom
delivers the scene's payoff line: 'All that's left is our friendship.'
Although Michael is miles away, we marvel at his operation, his
precision, his victory.

After Michael leaves New York for Sicily in *The Godfather*, Kay
visits the family compound. Tom won't let her in. The place is locked
down and guarded by Corleone soldiers. After the assassination
attempt in *The Godfather, Part II*, Kay is instead locked *in*; she can't
leave the compound – and it falls to Tom again to tell her why. In
both films, Coppola set Corleone family life in a compound (in New
York and then Tahoe) in part to make clear that the films are not
really or just about the Mafia: 'The whole idea of a family living
in a compound – that was based on Hyannis Port [home of the
Kennedys].'[22] The Corleones live well, well outside the law. That we
might say the Corleones live well *like* the Kennedys certainly supports
Michael's remark (voicing Coppola's treatise on gangster capitalism)
to Geary about hypocrisy.

The board meeting in Cuba

When yet another tonal cut takes us from dark to light, from dreary Tahoe to sunny Havana, we are meant to recognise a growing distance between Michael's family and professional lives: 2,700 miles as the crow flies to be exact. In a variation on a scene from the first film – one set in a sober boardroom where Vito negotiates Michael's return from Sicily – we meet 'a distinguished group of American industrialists', including Michael, Roth, and execs in the telephone and telegraph, mining and sugar industries, assembled to share in the spoils of an imagined new Havana. A local official assures the men: 'we won't tolerate guerrillas in the casinos or swimming pools'. But his assurance means less to Michael than a scuffle he has by chance seen on the streets involving a suicide bomber – a rebel willing to die for the cause.

A rooftop birthday party scene for Roth is highlighted by a cake in the shape of the island delivered with pomp to the assembled gangsters. Roth supervises slicing it into portions for his fellow industrialists. The gesture is meant to mark their success – acquiring,

Roth's rooftop birthday party

as Roth puts it, 'what we have always needed, real partnership with government'. But Michael's mind is elsewhere. Urged to make a speech, Roth establishes the order of succession, confirming that Michael will assume control upon his death. Michael doesn't think to say 'thank you'. And not just because he doesn't get much pleasure from money or property. Instead, he talks about the suicide bomber: 'I saw an interesting thing today …', and as we cut from Michael speaking to Roth's reaction (eyes cast down, worried), Michael adds, 'the soldiers are paid to fight, the rebels aren't.' 'What does that tell you?' Roth wonders. Michael: 'They could win.'

Making sure the other guests can hear, Roth dismisses the threat. He says there've always been rebels in Cuba, then pulls Michael aside and in a selective focus shot overlooking the ocean and the skyline: 'The two million never got to the island.' Later, in his hotel room, Roth says he's worried about Michael's commitment to the Cuba venture. Strasberg makes a neat choice here; he plays the scene shirtless so we can't miss the fact that Roth is old, slight, frail.

When he boasts: 'we're bigger than US Steel', as costumed, shot and played by Strasberg, we're not so sure. And neither is Michael.

Fredo arrives with a bag of cash. The $2 million. He's nervous; he's not so used to being trusted. But 'trusted' is not exactly what's in play here. Michael suspects that Fredo is the traitor. (We know he is.) Why else involve him in the deal? (Are we starting to think like Michael? Is that how we are meant to follow the story?) Michael asks Fredo if he knows Roth or Ola. (We know he does.) Fredo lies. His eyes dart around, looking everywhere except at Michael. It's a tell.

We cut to the brothers sharing a drink at an outdoor café. There aren't many scenes like this; quality time for family. Michael lets us in, briefly: 'It's not easy being his son, Fredo, it's not easy.' Fredo replies: 'Why didn't we spend time like this before?' The actor John Cazale, who plays Fredo, raises his voice and it cracks like an adolescent's. Weakness. Another tell. This is one of the few times since the attempted assassination we have seen Michael without his bodyguard – another reference to Fredo's weakness, perhaps.

Michael and Fredo having a drink in Havana

Coppola has used Tot, dressed in black even in sunny Havana, as a compositional element: his hat photographed in profile, a meta-reference (along with his nickname 'The Golem', from the 1920 German film of that name, directed by Paul Wegener) to the film's evocative expressionist lighting scheme. Michael shares a confidence: 'After this evening ... I'll be assassinated.' The garden scene again, in which Vito tells Michael that a family member will betray him. Michael vows to Fredo that he will kill Roth before Roth kills him. Fredo is confused: what does this have to do with him? He is about to find out.

Another meeting: Michael and Roth in Roth's Havana hotel room: 'Who had Frank Pentangeli killed?' Michael asks. Roth replies, tentatively: 'The Rosato brothers.' We had reason to believe it was Michael. Michael: 'Who gave the go-ahead?' Michael's beef appears to be procedural, but Roth's mind is again elsewhere. He wants the $2 million he's been told Fredo brought to Cuba. We've come a long way in a short time from the rooftop birthday party. Roth reminds Michael that murder is their business. He tells a story about Moe Green (a stand-in for the gangster Bugsy Siegel): 'Someone put a bullet through his eye ... When [Moe] turned up dead ... I didn't ask who gave the order because it had nothing to do with business.' Really, he didn't ask because he knew. Strasberg's voice cracks here, much as Fredo's had in the café scene. It undermines what he intends to be an ultimatum: 'I'm going in to take a nap. When I wake, if the money's on the table, I'll know I have a partner.' A prolonged silence highlights two cuts linking Michael's sight line and the object of his gaze, the ever-silent bodyguard.

Fredo leads an entourage out for a night on the town. Geary is in tow and tells Michael he's happy they 'can spend this time together'. Fredo is the night's entertainment director, but Michael has set the guest list, including especially the arrival of Ola, who walks into a two-shot of Michael and Fredo from the screen right foreground. We see Fredo in the middle ground facing the camera. He looks down and away. Another tell. Off screen we hear Michael

asking Fredo a second time if he and Ola have ever met. We cut to
another two-shot: a close-up of Fredo in profile looking away and
Ola in a medium shot facing the camera, awkwardly replying: 'We've
never met …'. Fredo can't meet Ola's eyes. Cut to Michael, seated, of
course; that's Pacino's tell that Michael is about to take control. In a
neutral medium shot captured in variable focus by a telephoto lens,
Michael observes the encounter between Ola and Fredo.

Fredo leads the group to a clandestine live-sex club. The sex
show begins but Michael isn't watching the stage. What makes this
guy tick? What turns him on? Michael exchanges a glance with his
bodyguard, the shots gorgeously composed in deep focus. Geary:
'Fredo, where'd you find this place?' Fredo: 'Johnny Ola told me …
He brought me here …'. We cut to Michael in close-up. The camera
holds on his gaze (at Fredo) – a gaze duplicated by the bodyguard,
who is held in variable focus. We cut to Fredo. He doesn't know he's
just made a terrible mistake. Back to the two-shot of Michael and
the bodyguard. Cue underscoring: we hear a brief violin figure mixed
with diegetic music, the music and ambient noise of the club. It is
a rare moment of sonic discord on a music track that is otherwise
lush and sentimental. Michael looks at the bodyguard. This is
how his mind works, or (as Roth put it) 'this is the business we've
chosen.' Identifying Fredo as the traitor greenlights the hits on Ola
and Roth. That we know what the bodyguard will do next is a sign
of our complicity, our insider's understanding of Michael's world.

In a variable-focus
two-shot, Michael
silently signals to
his bodyguard

Michael knows.
Fredo doesn't know
he knows ... yet

Cut to Johnny Ola on
the balcony of his
Havana hotel room

That we want it to happen, that we still want Michael to succeed, that we despise Fredo for what he's done – these are all sure signs of something else, something worse.

A medium shot of Fredo facing the camera shows him happy and oblivious with a showgirl on his arm. Michael's head is in his hand – an agonised gesture Fredo doesn't see. Cut to Ola on the balcony of his Havana hotel room. A music cue accompanies the arrival of the bodyguard from off screen. He strangles Ola from behind with a wooden hanger. We hear a siren in the distance, which subsides just as Ola does – a stagey, even corny bit of technique that is very *Godfather*, very Coppola. The murder is staged in a single full-figure theatrical shot. The music resumes to cue a second assassination attempt, but it cuts out when we discover Roth is not alone.

Coppola takes us in the meantime to 'La Gran Fiesta', the New Year's Eve party in Havana at which insiders in Fulgencio Batista's regime blithely celebrate at the very moment Fidel Castro's rebels take control of the city. Geary is on hand and in full party mode, too drunk (actually and metaphorically), like most of the American delegation there, to have seen this coming. Meanwhile, in another certain echo of the first film, the bodyguard tracks Roth to a local hospital where a second attempt on the old gangster's life is thwarted. We cut back to the party just as the clock strikes twelve. It will be a very different year for Cuba … and for Michael, Fredo and Roth as well.

We hear the Gran Fiesta band playing a jazzy version of 'Guantanamera', a patriotic song with lyrics by the Cuban poet José Marti, who died fighting the Spanish in the nineteenth century. The band doesn't know its history. That's the joke here. The lyrics tell of a 'sincere man' from 'where the palm trees grow'. The song was embraced by the rebels of the Cuban revolution, then later picked up as a peace anthem sung at the Vietnam War protests taking place at the very moment the film was produced. The song has been more recently adapted into tribal anthems at English football grounds. Culture is fluid, destined finally not to farce, but to meaninglessness.

Just as the New Year's Eve party is breaking up, Michael embraces Fredo and tells him there's a plane waiting to take them back to Miami and then grabs Fredo's face with both hands and kisses him full on the lips: 'I know it was you, Fredo. You broke my heart. You broke my heart.' Fredo backs out of the frame. Both men understand the meaning of things here: *Il baccio della morte* (the kiss of death). But here again Michael bides his time. Puzo and Coppola did not agree on what Michael should do about Fredo's betrayal. Puzo argued that Michael would never kill his brother. Coppola contended otherwise; although he appreciated the structural advantages of delaying its execution.

Il baccio della morte
(the kiss of death)

'I know it was you,
Fredo. You broke
my heart'

A cut from the brothers to a long shot of panicked Americans and Batista dignitaries feels at first like a cold shower – funny that a political revolution seems a letdown in contrast to the drama of these two brothers. Coppola shoots the fall of Havana in such low light that the violence is incoherent; it's just a background for Michael's smoothly executed exit. He's seen this all coming and has planned ahead; he did not in the end invest and lose money and he has had at the ready a private plane fuelled for his exit. On the way to the airport, Michael happens again upon Fredo. He implores his brother to leave Havana with him: 'You're still my brother.' But Fredo knows that won't necessarily protect him and disappears into the crowd blocked brilliantly by Coppola at the centre of the frame.

In a less ambitious narrative we would certainly be ready for the third act to take us home. But Coppola instead introduces a handful of new threads. Michael's sojourn in Cuba has played out uninterrupted. But his return to Nevada does not cue the expected dissolve to Vito's story and instead drops us into another meeting with Tom. Michael asks flatly: 'Kay know I'm back?' It's been nearly an hour since we've seen her. 'What about my boy? Get him something for Christmas?' Michael's tone is perfunctory. Tom is Michael's lawyer and half-brother but Michael treats him here like a personal assistant, a gofer. When Michael asks, 'Where's my brother?', Tom responds by talking about Roth – he is in Miami and the bodyguard is dead. Michael asks again about Fredo. Tom says, 'he must be somewhere in New York.' Michael tells Tom to contact Fredo, and 'let him know that everything's all right'. We know it's not – all right that is. But Tom has buried the lead; he tells Michael that Kay has miscarried. Michael's reaction is hard to read. He asks, 'was it a boy?' Tom veers off topic again – a nice touch in the script, as Michael likes things linear: 'Can't you give me a straight answer, anymore? Was it a boy?' Tom: 'I really don't know.'

We dissolve to young Vito – a medium long shot, his face in his hand. It's been a while. The head in hand gesture provides a link between young Vito and Michael and, more crucially, between young and old Vito, and by extension De Niro and Brando – generational talents from different generations. De Niro no doubt recognised the opportunity and the challenge when he went up for a role made famous by Brando. De Niro revered Brando – so much so that early in his career he sought out the acting teacher Stella Adler because Brando had worked with her.

During pre-production, De Niro tried to envision what a younger version of Brando's Vito might look like and worked extensively with the make-up impresario Dick Smith to get that right. He paid a visit to Brando's dentist, a Dr Dwork, to get fitted for a mouthpiece. He studied tapes of Brando's performance to create a continuity of mannerisms and gestures. He mimicked Brando's raspy voice, itself an impression based on recorded testimony of the real gangster Frank Costello at the Kefauver hearings into organised

Portrait of a young gangster

crime (more on the hearings later). '[The preparation] was fun,' De Niro remarked after the fact, 'a little like a mathematical problem.' Throughout a cautionary mantra prevailed: to maintain that 'thin line between identification and imitation'.[23]

Coppola admired De Niro, whom he had screen-tested for the role of Sonny in the first film. Footage from that test is included as a bonus to several different *Godfather* DVD packages, and it's a revelation: imagine the unhinged sociopath Johnny Boy from *Mean Streets*, a 1973 Scorsese film, as the Corleone heir apparent. After the part of Sonny went instead to James Caan, rumour has it Coppola offered De Niro the role of Carlo, Connie's husband. But De Niro turned it down, opting instead to take a bigger part in *The Gang That Couldn't Shoot Straight* (1971) – ironically, the film Paramount got Pacino out of in order to play Michael.

De Niro notoriously hates interviews, so much so it has become part of his mystique, what the film scholar Richard Dyer calls a star's 'discrete identity', the overlaps among biography, gossip and previous movie roles that impact upon our reading of movie star performances.[24] De Niro's reluctance to participate in Hollywood promotion has fuelled assumptions about his arrogance, about the strained seriousness with which he takes himself and his art. Neither assumption is true, although the reluctance does evince another nod to Brando, who famously disliked the Hollywood promotion machine. When the interviewer Lawrence Grobel talked with De Niro in 1989, the actor at one point turned the recorder off to make clear that he would not talk about his personal life. Pushed then to talk about the art of acting, De Niro turned the recorder back on but only to tell a joke, only to push back at the notion that he and his fellow Method practitioners take their work and themselves too seriously:

This guy hasn't acted in about 15 years, because he always forgets his lines, so finally he has to give it up. He's working in a gas station and gets a phone call from someone saying that they want him for a Shakespearean play – all he has to do is say, 'Hark! I hear the cannon roar!' He says, 'Well, God, I don't know.' The director says, 'Look, it'll be OK. You'll get paid and everything.' So he says, 'OK, I'll do it.' The play has five acts and he has to go on in the third act and say, 'Hark! I hear the cannon roar!' That's all he has to do. So he rehearses it when he's in his apartment: 'Hark! I hear the cannon roar! Hark! I hear the cannon roar! Hark! I hear the cannon roar!' Every variation, every possible emphasis. They're into rehearsal, and he's got it written on his mirror: 'Hark! I hear the cannon roar! Hark! I hear the cannon roar! Hark! I hear the cannon roar!' And so on. Finally, comes opening night, first act, no problem. Second act, things go fine. Audience applauds. Stage manager says, 'You have five minutes for the third act.' He tells him to get backstage. His time comes, he runs out, muttering to himself, 'Hark! I hear the cannon roar! Hark! I hear the cannon roar! Hark! I hear the cannon roar!' And as he runs out, he hears a big brrrooooom!! Turns around and says, 'What the fuck was that?'[25]

De Niro told Grobel that he found Coppola remarkably intuitive and astute; 'an actor's director', a director of actors. 'He leaves you alone. A director has to leave you alone and trust you.'

Exterior: Coppola and De Niro ponder the next shot (Photo by Michael Ochs Archive/ Getty Images)

De Niro extolled Adler's mantra, which Coppola respected: 'Make [the part] your own ... your talent lies in your choice[s].' Be confident, do the research, go all in. Preparation, according to Adler, is part introspection, part observation, part improvisation. Asked how he prepared for the role of Travis Bickle in *Taxi Driver* (1976), De Niro joked: 'Well, I killed a few people.' Then: 'I got this image of Travis as a crab. To prepare for that, I swam around under water and looked at sea life. I don't know, I just had that image of him. You know how a crab sort of walks sideways and has a gawky, awkward movement?' The challenge of playing young Vito Corleone was for De Niro a 'mathematical problem', a matter of reprising Brando's character with the right balance of impersonation and nuance. In play as well was the not insignificant matter of delivering most of his lines in properly accented Italian. De Niro is not a native speaker; in fact, he learned Italian via Berlitz on the studio's dime. To simulate Vito's likely dialect, he worked with 'a Sicilian guy in California'.[26]

The dissolve from Michael talking to Tom about family matters to Vito at home in his New York City apartment is meant to keep us thinking about Fredo. We have last seen him as a middle-aged man set adrift in Havana, so when we cut to the past only to find Fredo as a baby, sick with pneumonia, crying off screen, the parallel is surely strategic, meant to imply predestination, fate – to remind us why the drama of succession has played out as it has. In a gorgeous deep-focus composition, Coppola exploits the multiple fields in focus in the frame to mark the division of labour in the Corleone household, as we see Vito silently watching his wife attending the baby. It delineates women's work in that subculture and moreover associates Fredo with the homemaker who dotes on him. He's a mama's boy and all that that connotes.

Vito is a passive observer at home but an active breadwinner on the mean streets of Little Italy. We cut to Vito transporting stolen goods. Fanucci bursts into the picture and shakes him down. In Italian, Fanucci admonishes him: 'You and your friends should show

Fanucci in his white suit

me some respect.' He wants a third of their take or he'll tell the cops and their families will be ruined. 'Now don't refuse me – understand, paisan?'

The shakedown prompts a meeting between Tessio, Clemenza and Vito, who alone ponders the obvious: why pay Fanucci? 'He's one person, we're three. He's got guns. We've got guns.' The final bit surely alludes to Tony Comante in *Scarface* (1932), assessing a rival and finding him wanting. Tessio and Clemenza fear Fanucci, so they agree to let Vito handle him. Interesting that within minutes of seeing why Fredo will never be the Don, we see that Vito from the outset had the right stuff.

Another meeting. Outside a ragtag marching band plays the 'Star Spangled Banner'. Something essentially American – a macho pissing contest over power, money – is about to take place, a meeting in short order punctuated, settled finally by an act of violence. In a dimly lit café, Vito sits down with Fanucci, a dandy dressed in a ridiculous white suit. Fanucci wants $600. Vito gives him $100. (Clemenza and Tessio have given Vito $400. We know that. Fanucci doesn't.) 'You've got balls, young man,' Fanucci affirms, and offers Vito a job working for him. A gorgeous chiaroscuro shot highlights Vito's eyes as they follow Fanucci's theatrical exit; he's sized up the competition and figures he can beat him.

Outside the street festival continues. Coppola intercuts Fanucci parading about with Vito dashing across the roof of an apartment building where he has hidden a gun. A subjective camera allows us to see what Vito sees (Fanucci) so we share in the exhilaration of the moment. A low-angle shot on an apartment building stairway sets up another subjective shot; we see what Vito sees as he peers down the steps, anticipating Fanucci's approach. Vito partially unscrews the hallway light bulb – a meta-reference to Willis, regarded by his peers as 'the Prince of Darkness' for his penchant for working in low contrast, perhaps, as it is the scene's primary light. The band stops playing long enough for us to hear a priest offering a benediction – another echo of the baptism montage.

Coppola on a rooftop shooting the street festival scene

Vito assassinates Fanucci

The band resumes. Coppola is playing with sound fields again and not sticking consistently to diegetic or non-diegetic sound, to sounds that can be heard in the scene and sounds that comment upon it. We see Vito wrap a white towel around his hand as he lurks in the dark – a neat touch as the towel conceals his gun. We cut to the priest outside blessing the parishioners one by one. Fanucci stumbles for his keys, then (and we can hear it) taps the loosened light bulb. It flashes on and then off again. Vito, gun drawn, appears and then disappears. *Carpe diem*. The aesthetics of this murder convince us killing can be accomplished with style and, by extension, with meaning. Vito's and Fanucci's eyes meet. 'What have you got there?' Fanucci can't fathom what's about to happen, which is why it can happen. Vito fires twice. Fanucci falls dead. (Another nod to Tony in *Scarface*, who advises, miming with his hand the firing of a pistol: 'Do it first. Do it yourself. And keep on doing it.') The towel catches fire, a neat effect, which cues a cut to fireworks. ('Ding, dong the witch is dead.') The sound mix and cutting strategy allow for the analogy between events: the *festa* and the murder. And as we read more closely: among what the town celebrates, what the priest says and what Vito does. Much as the priest's benediction at the baptism of Michael's godson anoints Michael as the CEO of the New York mob in *The Godfather*, the music and the accompanying procession here mark the advent of the Corleone family patriarchy, the advent of the Corleone crime family.

A surprising, and I think unnecessary, cut back to the landing shows a gun shoved in Fanucci's mouth. A third bullet makes sure. ('Keep on doing it,' I suppose. But it does detract from the spectacle. It does remind us of the brutality previously downplayed in the *mise en scène* and editing scheme.) Vito reaches into Fanucci's pocket to recover his $100, then disposes of the gun and rejoins the festival. The sequence ends as Vito rejoins his family. There are three boys on the stoop of their tenement and we know just who they are. Vito speaks to the youngest: 'Michael, your father loves you very much.' Rota's 'Godfather Waltz' plays on the soundtrack: the difficult matter of succession is already in play.

A Corleone family portrait

Vito's assassination of Fanucci has taken us away from Michael's story at a crucial moment. When we cut to black, then back to the light of a snowy winter's day in Tahoe, it is clear these cuts back and forth are meant to enhance the suspense. We watch one narrative awaiting, still thinking about the other. Michael pauses to ponder Anthony's motorised toy car, the gift we gather Tom bought for the boy. A moving camera takes us through an empty house and ends as Michael pauses at a doorway where we see Kay sewing. She doesn't acknowledge his arrival. And he doesn't say hello. There's trouble in paradise. And we don't know the half of it.

A sound bridge marks an abrupt transition to a Senate hearing – a messy business problem that has come at Michael (and at us) quite out of nowhere. Whatever will become of Michael and Kay? We will have to wait on that. Meanwhile, Willi Cicci, a confederate of Pentangeli's and a Corleone soldier, is on the stand. This is Coppola's reimagining of the Kefauver hearings – 'The Special Committee on Organised Crime in Interstate Commerce'. And in this reimagining,

Willi Cicci at the Senate hearing

Michael is the committee's primary target, much as the likes of Mickey Cohen and Frank Costello had been at the real thing. The chronology of events here is a bit off – history made to suit Coppola's Corleone family melodrama. Batista fled Cuba for the Dominican Republic on New Year's Day 1959, with Castro taking control a few weeks later. The Kefauver hearings were staged in fourteen cities across the US in 1950 and 1951. In the real world, the two events were not really connected. They are here.

Cicci and Pentangeli have opted to breach *omerta* – the Mafia code of silence – because they believe Michael has betrayed them … because Roth has orchestrated things to suggest that he has. They rat as revenge. In doing so they betray a way of life that has given their lives meaning and shape. And we hate them for it. Such is the undertow of Coppola's gangster epic.

To portray the Senate committee chairman, Coppola cast the newspaperman and screenwriter William Bowers. Neither Bowers nor the playwright Michael Gazzo (who plays Pentangeli) had had much experience on screen but both do well to fit in with the otherwise all-star cast. Gazzo for sure looks the part of an old-school Mafiosi; his gravelly voice (like Brando's Vito) and accented English (along with his ability to transition easily from English to Italian and then back again) added authenticity, local colour even. Bowers in fact looks nothing like Kefauver, although few filmgoers were likely to know that. He looks more like J. Parnell Thomas, the chair of the House Committee on Un-American Activities, and the hearings scenes resemble that investigation more than Kefauver's, but Bowers nonetheless captures perfectly the Tennessee senator's air of Southern Baptist self-righteousness. In the autumn of 1950, Kefauver, the former maths teacher and Yale-educated lawyer, had presidential ambitions. And the optics of the Mafia hearings were quite perfect for him, as the senator embodied a WASP American repulsion for the ethnic gangsters he hauled in to testify, describing the Jewish gangster Cohen to a journalist as 'a simian figure, with a pendulous lip, thinning hair, and spreading paunch …'. The description was not inaccurate, but it is hard to miss that Kefauver was repulsed by Cohen's Jewishness. He (like Geary early in *The Godfather, Part II*) despised Cohen's masquerade, the gangster's pretences to nouveau-riche opulence, remarking on his 'sharp' clothing, including 'a suit coat of exaggerated length, excessively padded in the shoulders, and a hat with a ludicrously broad brim'.[27] Kefauver dressed like a middle-class businessman, like a small-town Baptist minister.

Cued by Rota's 'Godfather Waltz' we cut to Michael walking alone at the Tahoe estate and then to another meeting, as he sits down with his mother – another digression meant to make us wait, meant to mount the suspense. They converse in Italian; here, a secret language befitting an ageing aristocracy, and also a reminder of *la via vecchia*, the language of the Old World. Michael: 'Tell me something … What did Papa think … deep in his heart? He was being strong, strong for his family. But by being strong for his family, could he … lose it?' Mama Corleone thinks she knows what's on her son's mind: 'You're thinking about your wife … about the baby you lost. But you and your wife can always have another baby.' And then she assures him: '… you can never lose your family'. As in the garden scene in the first film to which this dialogue alludes, Michael listens attentively only to realise that what worked for his parents doesn't really apply to him. He concludes the meeting by saying, 'Times are changing.' The garden scene is capped by the line, 'There wasn't time,' which implies the same thing.

This reference to times changing cheekily cues a cut back to the past – a calculated risk, as things are so surely coming to a crisis point in Michael's narrative. Another dissolve takes us from Michael screen left to Vito – a bit older now, sporting a moustache – screen right. The effect casts the characters and the actors briefly face to face. (Filmgoers would have to wait for Michael Mann's 1995 cop-thriller *Heat* to see Pacino and De Niro in a scene, and on a set together, face to face.) Unlike Fanucci, the imperious dandy in a white suit whom he succeeds, Vito is Little Italy's unpretentious monarch, dressed in a rumpled suit, his ethos rooted not in an embrace of

Pacino and De Niro,
for a fleeting moment,
face to face

the accoutrements of wealth but in the proletarian ideals of hard
work. In look and manner, he projects Old World restraint, all the
while embracing the benefits *and* responsibilities of overseeing a
neighbourhood, reasonably dubbed 'Little Italy'.

Coppola introduces the nascent Corleone family business with
a vignette involving Mama Corleone. And with her as our guide, we
see how at first the family business and business of family once upon
a time intersected unproblematically. Mama escorts an acquaintance
to Vito's office. This woman she says is being evicted because she has
a dog. Vito agrees to intercede. Cut to Signor Roberto, the landlord,
getting a haircut, complaining about his unruly tenants who 'break
the windows [and] dirty the floors'. Vito confronts him and makes an
offer – a rent increase that he will personally pay in secret. But when
he says, 'and she keeps the dog', Roberto incautiously threatens Vito:
'Watch out or I'll kick your Sicilian ass right into the street.' Vito
presses some cash into Roberto's hand. The landlord muses aloud,
'what a character', and a comic bit of music colours the scene.
We know something Roberto doesn't … that the joke is about to
be on him.

Later that day, the landlord ventures to meet Vito in his office.
Outside we for the first time see the Genco Importing sign – a mark
of Vito's success and a winking reminder of the business he's actually
in. Vito stands outside the establishment proud of what the sign
means (prosperity) and what it masks (that real business he's in – his,

Vito and the landlord, Signor Roberto

per the senator from Nevada, masquerade). Inside we see the Virgin
Mary with the baby Jesus on the wall beside Vito. The set decoration
recalls Clemenza's basement retreat where he trains Michael in the
art of assassination; while the older gangster warns of 'pain-in-the-
ass innocent bystanders', we can't miss the picture of the Pope beside
them. Roberto knows by now he has made a mistake. And he is so
nervous to right things, he can't figure out how to open the door.

The comic vignette dissolves to a more serious setting: Michael
testifying at the hearing. The committee chair endeavours to conflate
family and business but Michael admonishes him, noting that if
he is called 'godfather', it is a personal/family/Italian thing: 'one of
affection, one of respect'. Geary is on the committee and can't wait
to get out of the room. He interrupts the proceedings to endorse
Michael's remark about godfathers, to make clear that the Mafia
hearings are 'in no way a slur' on Italian Americans in general. Some
of his best friends (including, albeit unacknowledged, Michael) are
Italian, he says, then exits.

Michael with Tom and Kay at the Senate hearing

The chair asks Michael if he is the head of 'the most powerful crime family' in the country. Michael replies, 'No.' The lie cues a cut to Kay, seated behind him, her eyes cast downwards. Michael then denies killing Sollozzo and McCluskey, murders we've seen him commit. He's then asked if he ordered the murders of the leaders of the five families. We've seen those killings too and we know Michael was behind them. But again, 'No.' Another committee member asks about Michael's Las Vegas casino holdings. Michael replies: 'I own some stock in some of the hotels there, but very little.' Tom leans over and whispers in Michael's ear. Michael puts his palm over the microphone – a prerequisite gesture at hearings, especially in the movies – then adds, at his attorney's suggestion: 'I also have stock in IBM and AT&T.'

We root here for Michael to quite literally get away with murder, a subject positioning that marks a change in the crime picture and in the culture that consumes it. In the 1930s crime films that established the genre – *Little Caesar* (1931), *The Public Enemy* (1931) and *Scarface* – the ever-colourful gangsters are in the final reel subdued by law enforcement, who are in these films depicted by contrast as rather colourless working-class Americans. The Production Code, which frankly reflected public attitudes about law enforcement, saw to that. In the *Godfather* films, the police are of minimal relevance – a reflection as well of the times. Michael has plenty of enemies, but they are most all of them men like him: gangsters and businessmen, gangsters posing as businessmen, businessmen behaving like gangsters. In *The Godfather*, Michael has two significant encounters with one cop, McCluskey, who punches him in the jaw outside the hospital where Vito is recovering from the assassination attempt. A while later, Michael puts a bullet in McCluskey's neck, tying up his first loose end.

Michael indulges a brief exile in Sicily after the murder, only to return to New York fully exonerated as McCluskey is revealed to be dirty (which he in fact was). That law enforcement as an institution might not be so honest and fair and that law enforcers might be corrupt and needlessly violent, were notions endemic to the 1960s counterculture out of which Coppola's film emerges, an attitude first evident in Arthur Penn's 1967 crime feature, *Bonnie and Clyde*, a film Coppola alludes to quite obviously in the scene of Sonny's murder at the Jones Beach tolls. In *The Godfather, Part II* problematised notions of crime and punishment are evidenced throughout, characterised repeatedly in Michael's moral relativism – here again, 'the same hypocrisy' applies. Such a cynical view of law enforcement proved remarkably attractive to young American filmgoers at the time, as it resonated profoundly with scenes of protests against the Vietnam War and for civil rights, public demonstrations of discontent that were met frequently with violent police reaction.

The hearing ends as Michael reads a statement into the record. It resounds with the same logic used by Nixon's dirty tricksters, the shamed ex-president's dark-ops entourage, but yet we can't help taking sides – ironic, really, because while he says the committee has no proof linking him to organised crime, we certainly do (but we just don't care):

In the hopes of clearing my family name, in the sincere desire to give my children their fair share of the American way of life without a blemish on their name and background, I have appeared before this committee and given it all the cooperation in my power. I consider it a great dishonor to me personally to have to deny that I am a criminal. I wish to have the following noted for the record. That I served my country faithfully and honorably in World War II and was awarded the Navy Cross for actions in defense of my country. That I have never been arrested or indicted for any crime whatsoever ... that no proof linking me to any criminal conspiracy, whether it is called Mafia or Cosa Nostra or whatever other name you wish to give, has ever been made public. I have not taken refuge behind the Fifth Amendment, though it was my right to do so. I challenge this committee to produce any witness or evidence against me, and if they do not, I hope they will have the decency to clear my name with the same publicity with which they now have besmirched it.

Not taking the Fifth makes for drama – Michael's real-world counterparts knew better when they were hauled in by Kefauver – but at that moment it seems like bad legal advice as the lies he tells put him on the hook for perjury. Frankie Pentangeli is alive. That revelation prompts another meeting: Michael, Tom and Neri. Michael: 'How'd they get their hands on him?' Tom: 'Roth ... he played this one beautifully.'

That meeting prompts another: Michael and Fredo. A gorgeous high-angle long shot shows the brothers at the window overlooking the snowy lake. A momentous setting to be sure. Fredo slouches in his chair, showing his soft belly to the alpha male, his kid brother. Fredo confesses – it's a neat match for the scene in which Michael gets the truth from Carlo before he kills him in *The Godfather*:

I haven't got a lot to say ... I was kept pretty much in the dark ... I didn't know it was going to be a hit, Mike. I swear to God, I didn't know it was going to be a hit. Johnny Ola bumped into me in Beverly Hills and said he wanted to talk. He said you and Roth were in a big deal together and that there was something in it for me.

'He said there was something in it for me'

We cut to Michael, again in profile. It is impossible to read his expression; but this is a business meeting, so emotions, Michael knows, are not so useful. The camera lingers on Michael as Fredo continues: 'He said you were being tough in the negotiations but if [we cut back to Fredo] they could get a little help and close the deal fast it would be good for the family.'

Michael is incredulous. 'You believed that story? You believed that?' Fredo: 'He said there was something in it for me. On my own.' We cut back to a two-shot; Michael standing now, Fredo sitting as if pinned to his chair. 'I've always taken care of you, Fredo,' Michael says. The line sets Fredo off: 'Taken care of me! You're my kid brother! ... I am your older brother, Mike, and I was stepped over.' Michael: 'It was the way Pop wanted it.' Fredo: 'It ain't the way I wanted it. I can handle things. I'm smart. Not like everybody says. I'm not dumb. I'm smart and I want respect.' *The Godfather* considers a father and three sons. *King Lear*, with boys. (Given the patrilineal succession, Connie doesn't figure.) Each of the three boys offers a different version or expression of American masculinity. That Michael – the quiet, serious, smart one – succeeds in more than one common use of the term marks a victory for his understated machismo, that of a controlled and directed man of patience well suited to *la via vecchia*.[28] Michael was, all things considered, always the only son for the job.

Like the scene with Carlo, Fredo's confession serves only to seal his fate. Fredo (slumping again): 'The Senate lawyer … He belongs to Roth.' Cut to a low-angle medium shot of Michael, looking down at Fredo. Here again Coppola's theatrical blocking is spot on:

Fredo, you're nothing to me now. You're not a brother. You're not a friend. [Cut to Fredo reclined still.] I don't want to know you or what you do. [Cue music; back to Michael.] I don't want to see you at the hotels. I don't want you near my house. When you see our mother, I want to know a day in advance so I won't be there. [Back to Fredo.] You understand?

We cut back to Michael as he makes a theatrical exit. Fredo, left alone still slumped in the chair, calls his brother's name.

Michael leaves the room and moves on. A cut takes him to another meeting where, in a chilling affectless monotone, Michael tells Neri: 'I don't want anything to happen to him while my mother's alive.' We hear a pulse beat on the music track as there is still some business Michael needs to attend to – serious business he will perform quite magically behind the scenes. The pulse beat forms a sound bridge to Pentangeli escorted from an army camp to the Senate. 'Ten to one shot he takes the Fifth and I lose,' Pentangeli moans to his minders. 'My life won't be worth a nickel after tomorrow … Some deal I made, jeez.' Still, when he walks into the Senate chamber, Pentangeli is his usual garrulous self. In medium close-up, he looks around and remarks out loud, 'there's Willi Cicci …'. And then, suddenly, his countenance changes as we see what he sees: Michael.

But the continuity cut from Pentangeli looking, his face falling, to what he sees is a misdirection; after all, he knew Michael would be there. Standing behind Michael is a little old man in an old-fashioned string tie. Coppola holds on the old man as, ignoring the men who frisk him, he looks back at the camera and by implication at Pentangeli. Coppola cuts back and forth again as their eyes meet and then back and forth again, a wordless exchange, with the old man in

Pentangeli's brother enters the hearing room

close-up and Pentangeli in a medium long shot. Following the logic
of the cuts and the camera placement, we can see that the scene is
getting away from Pentangeli, and that the old man is the reason why.
No longer so animated, Pentangeli is blocked a foot or so away from
his attorney, who is seated. The lawyer we surmise is now irrelevant.
Pentangeli looks down at the floor – a simple gesture that tells us he
knows he's been beaten.

Pentangeli is asked where he lives. He jokes: 'I live in the army
barracks with the FBI guys.' A committee member displays a poster:
'The Michael Corleone Crime Family'. Michael whispers in the
old man's ear. Asked by the lawyer if he worked for a crime family
headed by Michael Corleone, Pentangeli lies: 'I don't know nothing
about that. Oh, I was in the olive oil business with his father, but that
was a long time ago.' As the committee's case against Michael falls
apart, the identity of the old man is revealed: he's Frankie's brother,
flown in from Sicily to lend, as Tom glibly explains, 'support in his
time of need'.

Pentangeli on the stand

Back at the hotel in DC, Kay says what we have been thinking: 'I always knew that you're too smart to let any of them ever beat you.' Our rooting interests are so with Michael at this point, we resent her refusal to take pleasure in his victory. Kay has been planning while he and we have been elsewhere – it is interesting how much of what gets done in this very long film happens while we (and while certain key characters) are paying attention to something else. Her plan is a clean and swift goodbye, but she fumbles her advantage; she can't resist asking him one last time about his business: 'What really happened with Pentangeli, Michael?' She doesn't need to know, but Michael is for the moment happy to talk business.

A loud argument ensues and Coppola offers perspective by cutting from the hotel room to the hallway where Anthony and Mary await its conclusion. The implication is they have heard fights like this before. Back inside, Michael asks, 'Kay, what do you want from me?' It's not a question really, because Michael has no intention of providing satisfaction. 'Do you expect me to let you go?

Kay and Michael argue

Do you expect me to let you take my children from me?' Rhetorical questions. We cut to Kay in a medium close-up looking down at the floor. Michael notes the submissive gesture (much as he read Fredo's slouch) and presses the advantage.

Although it is at this moment unclear why, Michael tries to reel Kay back in. He promises: 'I'm gonna change.' He says it twice, as if repeating it might make it true. But when he says they can try again to, as his mother suggested, have another child, Kay, who has never had the chance to say or do much in the film, makes the most of her one big speech:

Oh, Michael – Michael, you are blind. It wasn't a miscarriage. It was an abortion. [Cut to Michael in medium close-up.] An abortion Michael. Just like our marriage is an abortion. [Back to Kay.] Something that's unholy. And evil. [Back to Michael.] I didn't want your son, Michael. I wouldn't want to bring another one of your sons into this world. [Back to Kay, crying.] It was an abortion, Michael. It was a son, a son, and I had it killed because this must all end. [Back to Michael.] I know now that it's over. I knew it then. [Back to Kay.] There would be no way, Michael, no way you could ever forgive me. Not with this Sicilian thing that's been going on for 2,000 years.

Michael strikes Kay in anger and knocks her back onto the couch; it's not like Michael to act without thinking, and that may well be Coppola's point here. Kay has got to him, and that's not so easy to do. Pacino takes a moment to acknowledge the gravity of what's happened here – not so much the effect of the violence but his character's apparent and uncharacteristic loss of composure. His hands tremble, a quite literal referent to the fact of his character being shaken. Michael isn't sorry for hitting Kay. After all, he doesn't apologise. But he is sorry he hasn't played the scene so well. So he composes himself, tunes out the noise about Sicilian legacies, and focuses instead on what he can control. 'You won't take my kids …'. And he rather follows up on the threat. We don't see Kay for another half hour and then only to see her more calmly shut out of his and her children's lives.

A hard, flat cut (so, not a dissolve) takes us to a train in Sicily. The resolution of the meeting with Kay is left for the space between things, the ellipses, as Coppola detours back to the Corleone origin story. Things are again suspended in narrative and real time, but we can safely guess that Michael will follow through on the threat. Vito is in Sicily with the family. But it is not exactly a family vacation, at least not as we civilians might envision. When they reach Corleone, the town of his birth, lush underscoring cues the scene of his long-awaited revenge. Here as elsewhere, Rota's music undermines Coppola's rationalisations about romanticising the Mafia. Vito's car pulls up to an opulent estate. The music stops. Don Francesco needs to be stirred from his nap; he's old and nearly blind – no threat to anyone anymore. But Vito – and Michael inherits or learns this from him – can't abide unfinished business. He has waited a long time for this moment and guts Don Francesco, all the while whispering in his ear. This is personal. Not business.

The Corleone family vacations in Sicily

As the train leaves the village of Corleone, a dissolve takes us back to Tahoe in winter. Mama Corleone lies in state. Fredo and Connie embrace and as they walk away from the casket Fredo encounters Neri, who looks him in the eye but declines to speak, and then Tom, who is only slightly more forthcoming. Fredo: 'Where's Mike?' Tom doesn't hesitate: 'Waiting for you to leave.' Fredo: 'Can I talk with him?' Tom: 'Sorry, Fredo, no chance.' (He says the same thing to Tessio just before the old gangster is carted off for execution. The two scenes aren't so different. But Fredo doesn't know that.) A beautifully blocked three-shot – Tom and Fredo in the foreground; Connie in the middle-ground – lit in silhouette alludes to the earlier scene when Michael rebukes Fredo, 'you're nothing to me now.' There are reasons for that, too.

Connie goes to see Michael in Tom's stead. A long shot of Michael seated, head in hand – that familiar, repeated gesture. Mary and Anthony are in the middle ground quietly playing, barely visible thanks to Willis's low-contrast lighting. Connie enters in silhouette

'I'd like to stay close to home now if it's all right'

from the centre of the frame – a theatrical entrance into a theatrical set piece. She walks from foreground to background. We cut as Connie kneels at Michael's feet. It's a finely staged scene and we can't miss the significance of the blocking and of her quasi-ecclesiastical gesture of supplication.

We cut to Michael in a close-up, lit in chiaroscuro, as Connie says: 'Michael … [cut to a high-angle shot of Connie from Michael's point of view] I'd like to stay close to home now if it's all right.' A pregnant pause. Michael does nothing without thinking; he nods, yes. Captured in high angle, Connie tries to broker a peace between her brothers: 'Michael, Fredo is in the house with Mama. He asked for you and Tom said you wouldn't see him.' Connie tells the kids to go outside, but they don't move until Michael gives them the OK. The camera stays on Michael as Connie from off screen confesses – a mode of rhetoric rather freighted here. Still kneeling at his feet:

Michael, I hated you for so many years. I think I did things to myself, to hurt myself, so that you'd know that I could hurt you … you were just being strong for all of us the way Papa was … and I forgive you … can't you forgive Fredo? He's so sweet and helpless without you. You need me, Michael. I want to take care of you now.

Mafia wives, sisters and daughters don't get much to do in gangster films, and they seldom get much screen time. Like Kay, like

Mama, Connie pops in occasionally but there are long stretches of film time during which she is not on the call sheet, absences that are, frankly, seldom conspicuous. The actor Talia Shire, who plays Connie, is the director's real-life sister. In a 1976 *New York Times* feature, she recalled her unlikely route to *her* big break in her brother's big break movie. When she was young, she could never summon the confidence to tell her brother that she wanted to be an actor. 'I didn't want to hurt my relationship with him, which was tender and complex because I was the girl in the family.' When she secured an audition to play Connie, he was surprised she was *that* serious about her profession, as he so surely was about his. When she landed the part, he was happy for her. But he didn't think it was that much of a role. 'He saw Connie Corleone', Shire recalled, 'as a kind of maid.'

Although there hasn't been all that much written about Shire, certainly in comparison to the two male stars of the film, she is nonetheless (like them) among the most important actors in late-twentieth-century Hollywood thanks to supporting roles (are there any other kind of roles for women?) in two blockbuster franchises: *The Godfather* and *Rocky*, in which she plays Adrian, Rocky Balboa's soulmate. To play Connie, Shire (who studied drama at Yale, by the way – so she was never only or just Francis's sister) dredged up a useful sense memory:

I used to go alone [when I was young] to the Radio City Music Hall …
I'd stand in those long lines, and then when I finally got to the ticket booth,
I'd turn around and go to the end of the line again. There's a real thrill
in denial. My whole life's been that way.

When she was a teenager, if she thought she'd be late for school, she hid in the basement. She was deeply afraid of confrontation, of calling attention to herself. Years later, after she had become one of the biggest box-office stars in Hollywood, she was still too self-conscious to 'walk into a room if [she was] late'.[29]

Talia Shire on *The Godfather, Part II* set

Shire has over the years been dismissed as Francis's sister, the successful movie music composer Michael Shire's wife and after that the film producer Jack Schwartzman's wife, Sofia Coppola and Nic Cage's aunt, the actor Jason Schwartzman's mother. 'My career doesn't dominate the house,' she told the *New York Times*, not exactly complaining. 'You could walk in and not see anything to indicate I was in the acting business.'[30]

When Shire delivers her monologue on behalf of Fredo, Coppola alternates between close-ups of Pacino (who says nothing) and high-angle medium close-ups of her. The speech is more about Michael than Connie after all. Coppola ends the sequence holding on Connie in medium close-up as Michael's disembodied hand takes hers in the centre foreground of the frame. (The shot foreshadows Fredo's murder, in which Neri's hand, holding a gun, appears just before we cut away; the symmetry is pretty cheeky.) Connie matters finally because with this gesture Michael seems to affirm as much. Pacino's gesture and Rota's lush score *seem to* cue a change of heart. But we should know better – we should know that we cannot trust Michael's feelings because it is not clear he has any feelings to trust. We should know by now that Michael *has to* kill Fredo, much as he had to kill Sollozzo, McCluskey, Carlo, Moe Green, Ola and Pentangeli. Maintaining control over the family business depends on settling all, even really old, accounts, disposing of enemies even after they are already neutralised.

Accompanied by dramatic underscoring, a long tracking shot takes Michael to Fredo, who is seated alone. The music crescendos as Michael wordlessly takes Fredo's face in his hands for the second time in the film and embraces him. Rota's music affirms the scale and scope of things; this is not just any family reconciliation, because in fact it is not a reconciliation at all. Something very different is about to happen.

The scene at first implies Connie's influence as the family's succeeding matriarch. But with Michael, family matters (baptisms, lawn parties, funerals) obscure and in the end only delay the necessary business at hand. We cut from Michael's hands as they hold his brother in an embrace to his face in close-up. His eyes look up and we cut to what he sees: Neri in a medium shot. Neri acknowledges the gesture and then looks down because he knows what comes next (and now so do we); with Mama's death there is just one reason why Fredo is welcome back at the family home, a reason neither Connie nor Fredo anticipate.

Michael, Neri and Tom meet to talk about Roth, who, like the real-life gangster Meyer Lansky after whom he is surely modelled,

Michael embraces Fredo, then looks over at Neri (who does not need to be told what he will have to do)

has become a man without a country. Lansky's story is worth a brief digression here, as in 1974 he was again much in the news. After being refused asylum in Israel in the autumn of 1972 (just two years before the release of *The Godfather, Part II*), Lansky had returned to the US to stand trial for tax evasion – a trial, it is worth adding, that ended with his acquittal. (He was, in the end, 'too smart to let any of them ever beat [him]'.) The Jewish gangster lived another eight years in a modest house in Miami much like the one Roth inhabits in the film, leaving behind an estate worth less than $60,000 – a far cry from the fortune he was said to have accumulated. Like Roth, he risked and likely lost almost everything in Cuba in 1959.[31]

Michael has by this point neutralised Roth; plus, Roth is ill, Tom tells Michael, and will be dead within six months. A hit on Roth, who will be escorted to prison by US marshals, Tom insists, would be 'impossible … it'd be like trying to kill a president'. (Tom is a lawyer, so he always thinks of reasons *not* to do things. Michael pretty much never takes his advice.) Tom's remark landed with a thud in 1974, as conspiracy theories on the assassination of John F. Kennedy had by then widely touted Mob involvement in its execution and cover-up. Michael counters matter-of-factly with a chilling worldview: 'If anything in this life is certain, if history has taught us anything, it is that you can kill anyone.' Tom tells Michael that he has already won, and wonders aloud if assassinating Roth is worth it: 'Roth and the Rosatos are on the run. Do you want to wipe everyone out?' Michael replies, by then weary of Tom's persistent weakness: 'I don't feel I have to wipe everyone out, Tom. Just my enemies.'

That sorted, Michael returns to the issue of loyalty. He despises loose ends. 'You gonna come along with me in these things I have to do, or what? [a pregnant pause] Because if not, you can take your wife, your family, and your mistress, and move them all to Las Vegas.' These hard feelings have been brewing for a while. Tom laughs nervously, a smart choice by Duvall: 'Why do you hurt me, Michael?' Formal phrasing for such a personal question. 'I've always been loyal to you ... What is this?' We cut to an over-the-shoulder variable-focus shot with the camera placed behind Tom's head. Tom is out of focus and Michael, the object of his gaze, is seated, framed in a medium shot, in profile and in focus. The blocking is clever here; Michael is the one thinking clearly or, at least, his point of view is the only one that matters. Michael sits at an angle, offering Tom only his profile, extending the metaphor that he is revealing to Tom only part of the picture.

Outmanoeuvred, Tom asks, 'What is it you want me to do?' Again, the formal diction is remarkable. The next cut does not take us directly to the answer; it's a continuity cut all right, meant instead to combine and conflate loose narrative threads that have in common only that Michael wants them tied up. We cut to the lakeside and Fredo and Anthony, two damaged children idling outside the world of grown men. Fredo tells Anthony that he recites Hail Marys to help him get lucky and catch fish. The affirmations of religious piety recall the baptism scene and we know how that played out. Coppola is banking on that.

'Crime is today inseparable from its representation,' the screenwriter and film critic Alessandro Camon asserts. And in Coppola's *Godfather* films, Camon adds, both crime and its representation evince 'an aesthetic dimension'.[32] All three *Godfather* films climax with a montage – a montage of murders that convey precision and finality and a surfeit of style ... things markedly absent in most everyday dealings for most everyone in America. The montages cue our engagement *with* Michael, absent moral judgment, absent any sort of philosophical baggage. In *The Godfather, Part II* Michael's sorting of loose ends begins with Tom's comeuppance and ends (as we knew it would) with a handful of dead bodies.

Michael dispatches Tom to visit Pentangeli, who has gambled and lost. He has no choice but to accept the deal on offer: a ritual suicide in exchange for the safety of his family. Tom exits affirming the family promise: 'Don't worry about anything, Frankie Five Angels.' Just as Tom tells Tessio at the end of *The Godfather*: this is business, not personal.

The next piece of business *is* personal but not so carefully planned, although it also disposes of yet another person who is already neutralised. With Connie's help Kay has secretly visited the children. We arrive just as Kay is about to leave. She kneels to hug Mary and then begs Anthony to kiss her goodbye. He silently refuses.

Tom settles matters with Pentangeli

Connie gruffly intercedes – it's a neat hint that time is short. I'd wager this characterisation of Anthony was in 1974 a set-up for another sequel focusing on how the third Corleone generation might deal with the success made by the first. Kay remarks at one point that there's something wrong with Anthony, but it is hard to miss that what is wrong with Anthony is expressed in his sullen silence, which surely recalls young Vito, whom Anthony resembles physically as well. But sixteen years would pass before Coppola and Puzo would get around to *Part III*. In that film, Anthony-reconsidered became less a late-twentieth-century version of Vito than Michael. In *The Godfather, Part III*, what Michael wants for Anthony is what Vito had wanted for him: a legitimate career, fully independent of the business that had made the family fortune. In an early scene in the 1990 film, Anthony asks his father's blessing for his decision to walk away from a planned career as a corporate attorney to become an opera singer. In doing so he disappoints his father not by becoming a gangster (as Michael finally disappoints Vito) but by resisting a practical career as an attorney for a more speculative future in the arts, like some engineering student changing majors, come home to tell his father he wants to become a painter.

Michael appears in the doorway. In what at first seems a subtle sound gag, we hear birds outside singing. But the point isn't the birdsong and how it runs counter to the serious business of the scene, it's how quiet everyone is – so quiet we can hear the birds chirping outside. We cut to Kay in a medium shot, suggesting Michael's point of view, then quickly back to Michael in a medium long shot, suggesting hers. The uncomfortable silence persists as he walks past the children. We hear the floorboards creak – the sound engineer Walter Murch wants us to *hear* how quiet it is. With Kay captured in a medium shot over Michael's shoulder, Michael repeats the gesture that ends *The Godfather*, and closes the door in her face, yet again shutting her out of his life.

Kay endures a tragic character arc, although like Connie she is relevant always and only with regard to Michael. Diane Keaton

Michael shuts Kay out of his life, again

gets to explore a wide range of emotions in these final scenes. But the indulgence only colours her failure. The narrative – Michael's narrative – values control, restraint. Kay is for Michael a lot of different things: at first a rebellion against Sicilian expectations, then an expression of his modernity and potential legitimacy (his WASP better half), then a distraction (from the plans he hatches, from the things he wants or needs to do), and here finally an irrelevance (shut out of his life with barely a wasted movement).

Connie and Kay's failed struggle against an entrenched Sicilian-American patriarchy was in 1974 quite timely. The first two *Godfather* films reached US screens amidst a full flowering of the counterculture-era women's movement. In 1970, marches and demonstrations marked the fifty-year anniversary of women's suffrage. Kate Millet published *Sexual Politics*, a book so impactful it put her on the cover of *Time Magazine*. The first issue of *Ms.* magazine appeared in July 1972, at the very moment *The Godfather* was completing its first run. And *Roe v. Wade* made abortion legal the following year – the year before Kay's revelation in *The Godfather, Part II*. The first two *Godfather* films struck plenty of women as retrograde. For example, the feminist film historian Molly Haskell wrote that the two movies indicated 'a retreat that pull[ed] at the reins of progress', a retrenchment that implied that 'women on the threshold of a mass movement toward consciousness-raising, stock-taking and sometimes lonely self-reliance, were already nostalgic for the take-charge male'.[33] These women were ready to change course, get back into the kitchen and get out of their husbands' way. Wishful thinking perhaps for the men in Hollywood making these movies, but, as Haskell notes, timely nonetheless.

Kay can't help herself when it comes to Michael. She is introduced as his new WASP girlfriend at Connie's wedding, but by the time that party's over – that is, at the very start of the first film – she already knows plenty about the Corleone family. When Michael comes back from Sicily and courts her a second time, she agrees to marry him, although he is by then a widower, with wife #1 murdered in an attempt on his life. He's dressed like a movie gangster, attended by bodyguards who serve and protect. She knows he's spent time in exile and, assuming she reads the newspapers, and didn't everyone back then, she knows he's been accused of killing a policeman and a rival gangster in a restaurant. So why does she say, 'I do?'

Haskell finds Kay, 'the pretty New England schoolteacher', 'the WASP outsider', a 'simpering … dim presence'.[34] But to be fair, in *The Godfather, Part II* Kay does finally stand up to Michael, even if she knows deep down she can't win. 'This Sicilian thing has to end,' she says. And although it doesn't, and for our sins we don't really want it to – so seductive is the depiction of Coppola's royal family – she is in that moment not at all simpering, not at all subservient; she's just outgunned. Kay will never be Apollonia – the perfect Sicilian wife. She will never be like Michael's defiant grandmother (who takes a bullet for her son) or a reliable homemaker mother like Mama Corleone. But she stands up to Michael even as he says, 'you know what I'm capable of.' And she knows.

The casting of Keaton has over the years struck plenty of filmgoers as a mistake. The hard guys in *The Sopranos* sure think so. When the New Jersey gangsters who so like to recite dialogue from the first two *Godfather* films get to talking about Keaton and Kay, they are unforgiving, mocking on more than one occasion her tepid delivery of the 'our marriage is an abortion' line in her one big scene. It is meant to be funny in *The Sopranos* that real-world gangsters

The good wife: Mama Corleone during the family trip to Sicily

might identify and idealise the fictional versions of themselves in Coppola's films, but it is in fact a thing, as surreptitious FBI wiretaps on post-1972 mobsters have revealed.[35]

Coppola was sure from the outset that Keaton was right for the part. She in fact screen-tested with a number of potential Michaels, including Martin Sheen and James Caan, as *she* was always getting the job. And Coppola liked what he got from Keaton in the first film enough to expand Kay's role in the sequel and then expand it again in *The Godfather, Part III*. Coppola appreciated Keaton's gift for comedy, and endeavoured to exploit the lightness of being she brought to the role to counterpoint the ever-intense Pacino. He'd try much the same strategy when Winona Ryder pulled out of *The Godfather, Part III* and he cast in her place his daughter Sofia (a decision that prompted more bad press). As Mary, Michael's ill-fated daughter, Sofia Coppola, an amateur in her first big professional film, is awkward – appropriately, he figured, given the age of the character and her adolescent crush on her cousin, Sonny's illegitimate son

Vincent, played by Andy Garcia, fifteen years Sofia's senior and by then a veteran actor and seeming movie star.

Haskell struggles to appreciate Kay *and* Connie, whose narrative – as she squanders her inheritance and explores her sexual independence – transpires almost entirely off screen, mostly in the time that passes between the end of *The Godfather* (after Michael lies to her about killing her husband and she calls him 'a monster') and Michael's assertion of power at his mother's funeral. By the time Connie returns to Tahoe for the funeral, she has, we gather, got the youthful rebellion out of her system. With her mother's death, she accepts her succession to family matriarch.

Connie's sojourn away from the family is never shown to us. But we know she didn't find what she was looking for. She is in her own way like a lot of the 'mad housewives' that populate 1970s American cinema, women for whom the self-actualisation on offer turns out to be a trap, women for whom sexual and social 'freedom' is tentative and partial and finally unhappy. Haskell sees Connie as chastened at the end of the film because she rejects emancipation. And she dismisses Connie as a supplicant because she kneels to kiss Michael's ring. The supplication gesture, though, is something men are asked to do as well – just as the door shuts Kay out of Michael's professional life in *The Godfather*, Clemenza kisses Michael's ring – but Connie's rejection of the freedom she explored out on her own, as Haskell fears, undoubtedly carries a message of conservative reassurance.

On the other hand, it is worth noting that Connie bravely leaves the nest and then *decides for herself* to return to fulfil her legacy. Her narrative is thus not so different from Michael's. When she's gallivanting about with men who care only about her money, Michael tells her she disappoints him. And for his trouble, she reminds him he's not her father – he's not the man his father was. Michael doesn't retaliate for the slight and instead waits out her rebellion like any good patriarch – like his father waited for him. When he welcomes her back it is as a fellow avatar of *la via vecchia*, which in Connie's case means doing women's work suited to an Old World Sicilian family.

The door shutting on Kay cues (instead of caps) the climactic montage, which begins with a cut on sound – the sound of the winch on the floating dock hardware. Murch again. We see Michael alone in his study – so we are again in on his alibi, in some intellectual/imaginative way accomplices with a rooting interest in his success. A boat arrives at the dock. Anthony, Fredo and Neri get on board. Connie arrives and takes Anthony with her. Fredo does not seem to see where this is heading. We do.

We hear the sound of the boat motor. Murch mixes in an ominous chord on the music track. Cut to Roth in an airport terminal attended by armed guards prepared to turn him over to US marshals. For anyone who has seen the first *Godfather* film – and that was most everyone at screenings of the sequel in 1974 – it is hard to resist the promise here, the euphoria: we have finally arrived at the settling of scores. Cut to the exterior of an army barracks and then to a couple of FBI agents playing cards, minding Pentangeli. Exterior, Tahoe compound: leaves blow across the lawn. The camera pans and then tilts to reveal the house. Cut to a wider view of Lake Tahoe, steel grey under a low ceiling of clouds. Two men in a boat. Suspense, remember, is about suspending things in narrative and real time.

Back to the airport. Roth, like Lansky just two years earlier, is taken into custody for tax evasion. 'I'm a retired investor living on a pension,' Roth intones impassively, 'I came home to vote in the presidential election because they wouldn't give me an absentee ballot.' The moment of levity is interrupted as a man, a journalist we figure, walks purposefully towards Roth. But he's not a newspaperman. He's one of Michael's soldiers. And he has been sent by Michael to kill Roth. He succeeds, and then, trying to escape, he is gunned down by federal agents. The scene is staged and blocked to resemble Jack Ruby's murder of Lee Harvey Oswald – a not so subtle reference to Michael's remark about lessons learned from history, a reminder again of the persistent rumours concerning Mob involvement in the Kennedy assassination and the conspiracy to obstruct justice afterwards.

Back to the army base. One of the FBI minders pauses at the door. Pentangeli is dead – bleeding out in the tub. Exterior: Lake Tahoe. Ominous music is mixed underneath the dialogue track as Fredo recites the rosary to bring on the big fish. The boat drifts in the water. The camera closes in. We recognise Neri and Fredo, albeit in silhouette. The boat begins to drift off frame. We see Neri shift his weight as he disappears off screen. We see his hand drift back into the frame … holding a gun. We see Fredo, Neri's target. Back to Michael standing at the window looking out at the lake. This is a killing he wants to see. This is a loose end he needs to see tied up. We hear the gunshot and Michael hardly flinches. Ominous music accompanies a cut to Neri seated at the stern of the boat. We hear a seagull; it's that quiet again. Neri stands in the boat, a man out of place and time,

Fredo and Neri gone fishing

Such are the burdens of power: Michael witnesses the murder of Fredo

an old-school gangster from a 1940s noir … Jacques Tourneur's *Out of the Past* (1947) comes immediately to mind, set partly in Tahoe as well, featuring a riverside murder involving trench-coated hard guys, one in particular 'gone fishing with a 45'. We cut to Michael at the centre of the frame in low light. Such are the burdens of power.

The film doesn't end with Michael alone in apparent victory; too bad, as for what it's worth, that is the ending I'd have preferred. Instead, Coppola dissolves to a coda, a nostalgic vignette. In soft focus, we see Sonny introducing Carlo to the family: Fredo, Tom, Connie and 'this droopy thing here', Michael. Tessio arrives with a cake. Turns out, it is 7 December 1941 – Vito's birthday, inconveniently and coincidentally also the day the Japanese have attacked Pearl Harbor. Tessio: 'I understand 30,000 men enlisted this morning.' Sonny calls these men 'saps … Because they risk their lives for strangers.'

Michael doesn't agree – 'That's Pop talking' – and calmly announces he's enlisted in the Marines. A family argument ensues but it is interrupted as Vito is about to arrive. Brando is even here in a soft-focus coda, a structured absence. Michael is left alone at the table; ever the outsider. We dissolve to find Michael as a little boy on the train in Sicily. This is something from Michael's memory, a tender moment spent with his father. The coda is deeply ironic. Michael knows more now as an adult, experienced gangster than he knew at the time, as a child. He is remembering a family vacation but he has to know by now that a very different bit of family business – Vito's revenge for the murder of his mother – was the real reason for the trip to Sicily.

We dissolve finally to Michael alone on the lawn outside the Tahoe house, a foreshadowing of the original ending of *The Godfather, Part III*. The camera closes in until we're in a tight close-up, one side of Michael's face is lit, the other is in the dark – a signature Willis trick with light. The lush 'Godfather Waltz' cues the film's final fade to black, punctuating the sentimental, nostalgic coda.

3 Michael Corleone, Tragic Hero/Role Model

In 1971, when Coppola accepted the offer to direct *The Godfather*, he vowed to modernise the gangster film. 'The Godfather* is not a film about organized gangsters,' he told the press, 'but a family chronicle. A metaphor for capitalism in America.'[36] The first *Godfather* film revealed how bourgeois American institutions and aspirations – family ties, social mobility, the quest for personal security, the burdens of responsibility, friendship and religion – were inevitably undermined by the drive for financial success … a drive complicated for the Corleone patriarchs by the long-term goals of fiscal legitimacy and cultural assimilation. In *The Godfather, Part II*, the parallel narrative structure depicts separately and in comparison Vito's and Michael's attempts to balance the Sicilian code of *la via vecchia* – to be 'controlled and directed', to be 'a man of patience', to follow a code rooted in nostalgia and received notions of the old ways of the old country – with the demands of a more modern American business and family life.[37] *La via vecchia* enables and maintains Vito's success, but it becomes for Michael, at home and on the job, the heart of an existential crisis.

The *Godfather* films – as Coppola had promised they would – reinvigorated and reinvented the gangster film; fully post-noir, steeped in the socio-politics of late capitalism. 'The career of Michael Corleone was the perfect metaphor,' Coppola mused in a 1975 interview:

Like America, Michael began as a clean, brilliant young man endowed with incredible resources and believing in a humanistic idealism. Like America, Michael was the child of an older system, a child of Europe. Like America, Michael was an innocent who had tried to correct the ills and injustices of his progenitors. But then he got blood on his hands.[38]

When crossed or challenged, Michael reacts without remorse. He has, if not a taste for blood, a tendency to view bloodshed as a means to an end. He emphatically avenges the senator's attempted shakedown and makes him pay for the ethnic slur – that awful morning Geary wakes up beside a dead prostitute is the sequel's horse's head moment. Roth is murdered on Michael's orders and Pentangeli kills himself in exchange for Michael's promise to support his surviving family. No one gets a second chance to cross Michael. Not even Fredo.

La via vecchia outlines allegiances tied to family life; for Vito there is the family and then there is everyone else. For Michael, it is never so simple or easy. Tessio, a family member, is loyal to Vito. But once Vito dies, Tessio rejects blood-based loyalty and sides with a rival gangster for (he thinks) fiscal security. The double-cross compels Michael's more modern business model.

The Godfather ends as Michael kills his gangster rivals, which he accomplishes so expertly we admire the efficiency of his consolidation of power without caring much about the brutality it has required. Such is our admiration for his precision and decisiveness, such is our admiration for the cinematic sequence constructed and executed by Coppola. In *The Godfather, Part II*, Michael again establishes control by dispatching his enemies – Ola, Roth, Pentangeli – and by supervising the murder of a family member, Fredo. Per John Hess's excellent review of the film for *Jump Cut* in 1975: at the end of *The Godfather, Part II*, Michael is at once the most powerful and loneliest man in America. The film, Hess asserts, is an object lesson in the karmic cost of capitalist success. Michael has everything and yet he is still unhappy.

Michael wins, Hess opines, *because* he is a cold-hearted monster, *because* he is capable of fratricide without remorse.[39] 'He is', per the essayist Robert Warshow's brilliant analysis of the movie gangster, 'what we want to be [winners, successful people] and are afraid we may become [oh, it's so lonely at the top].' Had he lived long enough to see *Godfather*s one and two, Warshow may well

The quintessential Michael Corleone

have cringed at the ending of both films, at how so many filmgoers fail to be repulsed at the monster Michael has become. Warshow would have suffered the irrelevance of the morality (in) play. We are meant, Warshow insists, to reject the gangster's drive for success because we recognise through him that the pursuit of the American Dream is a trap, 'defined not as accomplishment or specific gain, but simply as the unlimited possibility of aggression'. The gangster is at once monstrous and fascinating, and we may well be attracted to his (in the 1930s films, briefly enjoyed) ability to live outside social norms and moral restraint. We reject the gangster finally because we must reject his unrelenting drive for success and the brutality that such success requires.[40] In Hess's Marxist reading of the film and Warshow's existential overview of the gangster picture, filmgoers can't possibly *want* the loneliness, the oblivion that will surely mark the gangster in the final reel.

    The Godfather, Part II is a period piece – two period pieces really – but it was nonetheless upon its release in 1974 profoundly

Michael Corleone, role model

tied to its time as well. It resonated with a deeply cynical post-Watergate zeitgeist, presaging the evolution of neo-liberalism, financialisation and globalisation. A new generation of filmgoers seem sadly to have misread this critique. For them, Michael, the cold-hearted and cold-blooded gangster businessman, has become, as the film historian David Thomson sardonically asserts, a postmodern antihero. 'Just as Michael presides over his world,' Thomson writes, 'we are masters of our dream, and it is a Corleone-like axiom that we can have anything we want – if we want it enough.'

A few years ago, I taught *The Catcher in the Rye* in a class on American youth culture. Along with so many among my generation, when I read Salinger's book (back when I was about the same age as my college students are now) I empathised with Holden Caulfield's existential struggle. I was surprised and dismayed to discover that this new crop of late teens and twentysomethings had little patience for Holden's 'whining' – a view summarised neatly by a student who groused, 'why doesn't he just get a job?'

Often enough in my classes these days, students miss the point of Michael Corleone as well. They admire his sense of purpose, what Thomson ascribes as his 'pristine numbness … his coldness, his authority, his clarity, his sense of necessity'. For a lot of these students, the 'sleepless, sexless, tidy, deft, economical, heartless' monster that is Michael Corleone – this second-generation godfather of a second-generation criminal empire – is a role model peculiarly suited to the real world they are, so many of them, waiting to conquer.[41]

When Vito meets with Sollozzo in *The Godfather* and rejects the drug runner's proposal of limited partnership, he waxes philosophical: 'It don't make any difference to me what a man does for a living.' Vito views Sollozzo's drug business as 'a little dangerous' – ironic given what he too does for a living, and disingenuous as well, as he qualifies his seeming open-mindedness about what others do for a living by dismissing the Turk with a thinly veiled threat, wishing him luck, provided the drug runner's interests don't conflict with his. Vito's short-sightedness, his nearly fatal mistake as Sollozzo finds financing elsewhere and with Barzini's help attempts to assassinate him, no doubt fuels Michael's cynicism, his view that all modes of and routes to capital accumulation and political power are 'part of the same hypocrisy'. Michael would never have made the same mistake with the Turk – at least, he would not have judged his rival's endeavours as any more corrupt than his own.

When in *The Godfather, Part II* Michael (a bit out of character) dresses down Roth for greenlighting the hit on Pentangeli, Roth reminds him that murder is endemic to modern gangster capitalism, that when 'someone put a bullet through [his friend Moe Greene's] eye', he wasn't angry, and he didn't ask who gave the order (well, he knew it was Michael), because 'this is the business we've chosen'. It is a reminder to Michael more than a reprimand … Pentangeli was, per Roth, 'small potatoes' anyway.

For those inclined to embrace Michael's Darwinian propensities – 'I don't feel I have to wipe everyone out, Tom. Just my enemies' – for those inclined to take him on as a role model, there is still, I have to believe, a moment when common sense prevails, a moment when, despite pretences, Warshow is right about them (the gangsters) and us (civilians, moviegoers). Even as audiences today might want to idealise and identify with Michael Corleone (just as we idealise and identify with film characters in so many other films), there is still that moment (as there is in those other films) when we realise (per Warshow) that we are not him, that we are not like him, no matter how much we think we might like to be. At the end of *The Godfather, Part II*, Michael orders the murder of his brother and then watches its execution. He does so because the murder is necessary in the business he has chosen, or, and this may be the more accurate and tragic accounting, it is necessary to his prominence and power in the business that has chosen him. He does so (murder his brother, that is) because he can – and because, Coppola is betting, under these same or any circumstances, we can't.

Notes

1 Stephen Farber, 'They Made Him Two Offers He Couldn't Refuse', *New York Times*, 22 December 1974, p. C1.

2 Pauline Kael, '*Paint Your Wagon*: Somebody Else's Success', in Joseph Morgenstern and Stefan Kanfer (eds), *Film 69/70: An Anthology of the National Association of Film Critics* (New York: Simon & Schuster, 1970), p. 112.

3 Pauline Kael, '*The Godfather Part II*: Fathers and Sons', *New Yorker*, 23 December 1974. Available at: <https://scrapsfromtheloft.com/movies/the-godfather-part-ii-fathers-and-sons-review-by-pauline-kael/> (accessed 1 February 2022).

4 Charles Champlin, '"Godfather II": An Epic Expanded', *Los Angeles Times*, 17 December 1974, p. G1.

5 I outline this history elsewhere. See, for example: Jon Lewis, *The Godfather* (London: BFI, 2010), pp. 46–61.

6 Steve Rose, 'I promised Brando I would not touch his Oscar: the secret life of Sacheen Littlefeather', *Guardian*, 3 June 2021. Available at: <https://www.theguardian.com/us-news/2021/jun/03/i-promised-brando-i-would-not-touch-his-oscar-secret-life-sacheen-littlefeather> (accessed 1 February 2022). Littlefeather's speech is currently posted on YouTube at: <https://youtu.be/2QUacU0I4yU> (accessed 1 February 2022).

7 Mike Fleming, 'Francis Ford Coppola: How Winning Cannes 40 Years Ago Saved "Apocalypse Now", Making "Megalopolis", Why Scorsese Almost Helmed "Godfather Part II" & Re-cutting Three Past Films', *Deadline*, 13 May 2019. Available at: <https://deadline.com/2019/05/francis-ford-coppola-apocalypse-now-cannes-40-anniversary-megalopolis-scorsese-godfather-part-ii-re-cutting-godfather-iii-cotton-club-interview-1202613659/> (accessed 1 February 2022).

8 William Murray, 'Francis Ford Coppola: Playboy Interview', *Playboy*, July 1975. Available at: <https://scrapsfromtheloft.com/movies/francis-ford-coppola-playboy-interview/> (accessed 1 February 2022).

9 Michael Pye and Lynda Myles, *The Movie Brats* (New York: Holt, 1979), p. 81.

10 Louise Sweeney, 'The Movie Business is Alive and Well and Living in San Francisco', *Show*, April 1970, p. 82.

11 Pye and Myles, *Movie Brats*, p. 83.

12 Francis Coppola, 'On the Director', in Fred Baker (ed.), *The Movie People* (New York: Douglas, 1972), p. 67.

13 Marjorie Rosen, 'Francis Ford Coppola Interview', *Film Comment* 10, no. 4 (1974), pp. 43–9.

14 Lawrence Grobel, 'Al Pacino: The Playboy Interview', *Playboy*, December 1979. Available at: <https://scrapsfromtheloft.com/movies/al-pacino-playboy-interview-1979/> (accessed 1 February 2022).

15 Ron Rosenbaum, 'Al Pacino Out of the Shadows', *Vanity Fair*, October 1989. Available at: <https://www.vanityfair.com/hollywood/2018/04/al-pacino-october-1989-cover-story> (accessed 1 February 2022).

16 Ibid.

17 Ibid.

18 Ibid.

19 John Lahr, 'Caught in the Act: What Drives Al Pacino', *New Yorker*,

15 September 2014. Available at: <https://www.newyorker.com/magazine/2014/09/15/caught-act> (accessed 1 February 2022).
20 Murray, 'Francis Ford Coppola: Playboy Interview'.
21 Ibid.
22 Ibid.
23 Wayne Warga, 'Will Success Spoil *Godfather II*?', *Los Angeles Times*, 12 January 1975, p. R1.
24 Richard Dyer, *Stars* (London: Bloomsbury Academic, 1998), pp. 93–100.
25 Lawrence Grobel, 'Robert De Niro: Playboy Interview', *Playboy*, June 1989. Available at: <http://translatedby.com/you/robert-de-niro-playboy-interview-january-1989/original/?page=1> (accessed 1 February 2022).
26 Ibid.
27 Tere Tereba, *Mickey Cohen: The Life and Crimes of L.A.'s Most Notorious Mobster* (Chicago: ECW Press, 2012), pp. 152–61, 152.
28 See Alessandro Camon, '*The Godfather* and the Mythology of Mafia', and Vera Dika, 'The Representation of Ethnicity in *The Godfather*', in Nick Browne (ed.), *Francis Ford Coppola's* The Godfather *Trilogy* (Cambridge: Cambridge University Press, 2000), pp. 57–108.
29 Judy Klemesrud, 'Talia Shire: No Longer the Kid Sister', *New York Times*, 22 November 1976, p. 63.
30 Ibid.
31 See Robert Lacey, *Little Man: Meyer Lansky and the Gangster Life* (Boston: Little Brown, 1991), and T. J. English, *Havana Nocturne: How the Mob Owned Cuba and Then Lost It to the Revolution* (New York: William Morrow, 2008).
32 Camon, '*The Godfather* and the Mythology of Mafia', p. 74.
33 Molly Haskell, 'The World of *The Godfather*: No Place for Women', *New York Times*, 23 March 1997, p. H17.
34 Ibid.
35 See Selwyn Raab, *Five Families: The Rise, Fall, and Resurgence of America's Most Powerful Mafia Empires* (New York: St Martin's, 2006), p. 196.
36 Robert Evans, *The Kid Stays in the Picture* (New York: Hyperion, 1994), p. 220.
37 Dika, 'Representation of Ethnicity in *The Godfather*', p. 88.
38 Murray, 'Francis Ford Coppola: Playboy Interview'.
39 John Hess, '*Godfather II*: A Deal Coppola Couldn't Refuse', *Jump Cut* no. 7 (1975), pp. 1, 10–11.
40 Robert Warshow, 'The Gangster as Tragic Hero', *Partisan Review*, February 1948, pp. 240–4.
41 David Thomson, 'Michael Corleone, Role Model', *Esquire*, March 1997, pp. 60–2.

Credits

Mario Puzo's
The Godfather, Part II
USA
1974

Directed and
Produced by
Francis Ford Coppola
Screenplay by
Francis Ford Coppola
Mario Puzo
Based on the novel *The*
Godfather by Mario Puzo
Co-produced by
Gray Frederickson
Fred Roos
Production Company
Coppola Company

A Paramount Picture
© 1974 by Paramount
Pictures Corporation and
the Coppola Company.
All rights reserved
A Coppola Company
Production
Production facilities
furnished through
American Zoetrope,
San Francisco

Director of Photography
Gordon Willis
Production Design
Dean Tavoularis
Edited by
Peter Zinner
Barry Malkin
Richard Marks
Costume Design
Theadora Van Runkle

Associate Producer
Mona Skager
Music Composed by
Nino Rota
Additional Music
Composed/Conducted
by
Carmine Coppola
Sound Montage/
Re-recording
Walter Murch
Art Director
Angelo P. Graham
(as Angelo Graham)
Set Decorator
George R. Nelson
Make-up Artists
Dick Smith
Charles H. Schram
(as Charles Schram)
Production Manager
Michael S. Glick
Assistant Director
Newt Arnold
(as Newton Arnold)
Second Assistant
Directors
Henry J. Lange Jr
Charles Myers
(as Chuck Myers)
Michael Kusley
(as Mike Kusley)
Alan Hopkins
Burt Bluestein
New York Location
Supervisor
Ronald Colby
(as Ron Colby)
Production Secretary
Nanette Siegert

Casting
Mike Fenton
(as Michael Fenton)
Jane Feinberg
Vic Ramos
Location Coordinator
Jack English
Researcher
Deborah Fine
Unit Publicist
Eileen Peterson
Title
Wayne Fitzgerald
Hair Stylist
Naomi Cavin
Wardrobe
Marie Osborne
Eric Seelig
George Newman
Thomas Welsh
(as Tommy Welsh)
Marilyn Putnam
Nancy McArdle
Sandy Berke Jordan
(as Sandra Burke)
Assistant Editors
George Berndt
Bobbe Kurtz
Lisa Fruchtman
Sound Effects Editors
Howard Beals
James Fritch
(as Jim Fritch)
James J. Klinger
(as Jim Klinger)
Sound Montage
Associates
Pat Jackson
Mark Berger
Music Editor
George Brand

Special Effects
A. D. Flowers
Joe Lombardi
Location Assistants
Randy Carter
Mona Houghton
Melissa Mathison
Subtitler
Sonya Friedman
Sicilian Translator
Romano Pianti
Foreign Post-production
Peter Zinner
Camera Operator
Ralph Gerling
Camera Assistant
William Gereghty
(as Bill Gereghty)
Key Grip
Bob Rose
Gaffer
George Holmes
Production Recording
Charles M. Wilborn
(as Chuck Wilborn)
Nathan Boxer
Script Supervisors
John Franco
B. J. Bjorkman
(as B. J. Bachman)
Properties
Douglas E. Madison
(as Doug Madison)
V. R. Bud Shelton
(as V. Bud Shelton)
Location Auditor
Carl Skelton

[Sicilian Unit]
Production Supervisor
Valerio De Paolis
(as Valerio DePaolis)
Unit Manager
Mario Cotone
Assistant Director
Tony Brandt
Assistant Set Decorator
Joe Chevalier
Casting
Emy DeSica
Maurizio Lucci
Script Supervisor
Serena Canevari
Production Assistant
Bruno Perria
Miami Coordinator
Tammy Newell
**Senate Hearings
Advisor**
Edward Guthmann
(as Ed Guthman)
Music
'Senza mamma',
Francesco Pennino;
'Napule ve salute',
Francesco Pennino; 'Mr
Wonderful', Jerry Bock,
Larry Holofcener, George
Weiss; 'Heart and Soul',
Frank Loesser and Hoagy
Carmichael

Paramount Pictures
gratefully acknowledges
the cooperation of the
people of the Dominican
Republic for their help
in filming portions of
this motion picture.

Certain scenes filmed
at the Embajador
Hotel, Santo Domingo,
Dominican Republic.

uncredited
Art Direction
John Dapper
Hair Stylists
Edie Lindon
Dedee Petty
Painter
Eugene Acker
Leadman
Matty Azzarone
Props
Nick Caparelli
Greensman Gang Boss
Gerard Dery
Carpenters
Gary Fettis
Robert Hart
Property Master
Jerry Graham
**Assistant Property
Master**
Gary F. Kieldrup
Drapery Foreman
Bob Jepsen
**Construction
Coordinator**
John LaSandra
Construction Gang Boss
Claude F. Powell
Foley Artist
Kitty Malone
Boom Operator
Patrick Mitchell
Playback Sound
James Perdue
Ben Sobin

ADR Voice Casting
Maurice Schell
ADR Recordist
Mel Zelniker
Stunts
Phil Adams
Tony Amato Sr
Ted Grossman
George Robotham
Wally Rose
Stunt Gaffer/Stunts
George Sawaya
Dolly Grip
Pat Campea Sr
Grip
Johnie Carroll
Camera Assistant
Bob Edessa
Best Boy
Carl R. Gibson Jr
First Camera Assistant
James Glennon
Electrician
Lloyd Gowdy
Best Boy
Larry D. Howard
Electrician
Larry Keys
First Assistant Camera
Robert D. McBride
Still Photographer
Bruce McBroom
Electrician
Steve Pellant
Generator Operators
Arley Waters
Bill Williams

Wardrobe
Frances Kandelin
Harrison
Kent James
Cliff Langer
Wardrobe Assistant
Paul B. Schaeffer
Key Wardrobe
Ray Summers
Location Assistant
Jesse Wayne
Musician (Tuba)
Tommy Johnson
Musician (Flute)
Louise Di Tullio
Transportation Captain
James D. Brubaker
Drivers
Chris Haynes
Hugh Kelly
First Aid
Joe Catalfo
Welfare Worker
Shirley Deckert
Studio Executive
Robert Evans
**Production Assistant
(New York)**
Stephen A. Glanzrock
Publicist
Eileen Peterson
Stand-in
Paul B. Schaeffer

Thanks to
The producers would
like to thank James
Caan for his special
participation in this film

CAST
Al Pacino
Michael
Robert Duvall
Tom Hagen
Diane Keaton
Kay
**Robert De Niro
(as Robert DeNiro)**
Vito Corleone
John Cazale
Fredo Corleone
Talia Shire
Connie Corleone
Lee Strasberg
Hyman Roth
Michael V. Gazzo
Frankie Pentangeli
G. D. Spradlin
Senator Pat Geary
Richard Bright
Al Neri
**Gastone Moschin
(as Gaston Moschin)**
Fanucci
Tom Rosqui
Rocco Lampone
**Bruno Kirby
(as B. Kirby Jr)**
Young Clemenza
Frank Sivero
Genco
**Francesca De Sapio
(as Francesca de Sapio)**
Young Mama Corleone
Morgana King
Mama Corleone
**Marianna Hill
(as Mariana Hill)**
Deanna Corleone

Leopoldo Trieste
Signor Roberto
Dominic Chianese
Johnny Ola
Amerigo Tot
Michael's bodyguard
Troy Donahue
Merle Johnson
John Aprea
Young Tessio
Joe Spinell
Willi Cicci
Abe Vigoda
Tessio
Tere Livrano
Theresa Hagen
Gianni Russo
Carlo
Maria Carta
Vito's mother
Oreste Baldini
Vito Andolini as a boy
Giuseppe Sillato
Don Francesco
Mario Cotone
Don Tommasino
James Gounaris
Anthony Corleone
Fay Spain
Mrs Marcia Roth
Harry Dean Stanton
FBI man #1
James Murdock
(as David Baker)
FBI man #2
Carmine Caridi
Carmine Rosato
Danny Aiello
Tony Rosato
Carmine Foresta
policeman

Nick Discenza
bartender
Joseph Medaglia (as
Father Joseph Medeglia)
Father Carmelo
William Bowers
Senate committee
chairman
Joseph Della Sorte
(as Joe Della Sorte)
Michael's buttonman #1
Carmen Argenziano
Michael's buttonman #2
Joe Lo Grippo
Michael's buttonman #3
Ezio Flagello
impresario
Livio Giorgi
tenor in 'Senza mamma'
Kathleen Beller
(as Kathy Beller)
girl in 'Senza mamma'
Saveria Mazzola
Signora Colombo
Tito Alba
Cuban president
Johnny Naranjo
Cuban translator
Elda Maida
Pentangeli's wife
Salvatore Po
Vincenzo, Pentangeli's
brother
Ignazio Pappalardo
Mosca
Andrea Maugeri
Strollo
Peter LaCorte
Signor Abbandando
Vincent Coppola
street vendor

Peter Donat
Questadt
Tom Dahlgren
Fred Corngold
Paul B. Brown
Senator Ream
Phil Feldman
senator #1
Roger Corman
senator #2
Ivonne Coll
(as Yvonne Coll)
Yolanda
Joe De Nicola
(as J. D. Nicols)
Freddy, attendant
at brothel
Edward Van Sickle
Ellis Island doctor
Gabriella Belloni
(as Gabria Belloni)
Ellis Island nurse
Richard Watson
customs official
Venancia Grangerard
Cuban nurse
Erica Yohn
governess
Teresa Tirelli
(as Theresa Tirelli)
midwife
Louis Marino
young Michael Corleone

uncredited
Margaret Bacon
Al Beaudine
Jack Berle
Dick Cherney
Len Felber
Raven Grey Eagle

George Holmes
Shep Houghton
Kathryn Janssen
Alan Marston
Joe Pine
Al Roberts
George Simmons
Nico Stevens
Arthur Tovey
Wally West
Judith Woodbury
Senate hearing
spectators
Max Brandt
extra
James Caan
Santino 'Sonny' Corleone
Italia Coppola
Mama Corleone's body
Roman Coppola
Sonny Corleone as a boy
Sofia Coppola
child on ship
Victor Pujols Faneyte
Cuban guerrilla with
grenade
Julie Gregg
Sandra Corleone
Larry Guardino
Vito's uncle
Dan Harris
Victor Rizzi
(Connie's son)
Buck Houghton
senator with moustache
Karyn Jansen
Gianna Hagen
Ken Koc
waiter #1

Shô Kosugi
passerby with cap
pulled down
Gary Kurtz
photographer in court
Alan Lee
Klingman (casino owner)
Laura Lyons
guest
Thomas Mars
boy flautist
Richard Matheson
senator #3
John Megna
young Hyman Roth
Steve Peck
dancer at Lake Tahoe
party
Romano Pianti
gunsmith
Felipe Polanco
extra
Jay Rasumny
street vendor
Harrison Ressler
man in crowd
Hank Robinson
man guarding
Hyman Roth
Rhea Ruggiero
vaudeville dancer
Carmelo Russo
man who greets Vito
Filomena Spagnuolo
extra in Little Italy
Herkulis E. Strolia
Tahoe bandleader
Julian Voloshin
Sam Roth

Production Details
35mm
1.85:1
Colour (Technicolor)
Running time:
200 minutes
Length: 17,979 feet
MPAA certification
no. 24038

Release Details
US premiere on
12 December 1974
in New York City; US
theatrical release
20 December 1974 by
Paramount Pictures
UK theatrical release
15 May 1975 by
Cinema International
Corporation